Reb Noson of Breslov

Entering the Light

Prayers to Experience the Joy & Wonder of Shabbat and Yom Tov

Translated and Annotated by
Dovid Sears

Published by
Breslov Research Institute
Jerusalem/New York

COPYRIGHT © 2007 BRESLOV RESEARCH INSTITUTE

ISBN 978-1-928822-14-1

No part of this book may be translated, reproduced, stored in any retrieval system or transmitted, in any form or by any means, electronic, mechanical, photocopying, recording or otherwise, without prior permission in writing from the publisher.

First edition

For further information:
Breslov Research Institute, POB 5370, Jerusalem, Israel
or:
Breslov Research Institute, POB 587, Monsey, NY 10952-0587

www.breslov.org
e-mail: info@breslov.org

Printed in Israel

This publication
is dedicated to the

Saka Family

May the merit of Rebbe Nachman
be with you at all times for
good health and prosperity.

Dedicated to the memory of

Rabbi Aryeh Kaplan

Aryeh Moshe Eliyahu ben Shmuel
1935-1983
(14 Shevat 5743)

Rabbi Kaplan's translation of *Rabbi Nachman's Wisdom* in 1973 brought the teachings of Breslover Chassidut to the English-speaking public for the very first time. Next, Rabbi Kaplan produced a brilliant translation of *Outpouring of the Soul: Rabbi Nachman's Path in Meditation*; a translation and commentary of *Rabbi Nachman's Stories*; and a definitive biography of the Rebbe, *Until the Mashiach*. With Rabbi Kaplan's untimely passing at the age of forty-eight, the Torah world lost one of its finest scholars.

Table of Contents

Preface 11

Shabbat 15
1. Receiving Shabbat with Joy 16
2. Spiritual Exodus 18
3. The Shabbat State of Mind 19
4. Getting Ready for Shabbat 21
5. Extending Shabbat 23
6. Shabbat Peace 25
7. The Secret of Faith 27
8. The Day That is Entirely Shabbat 31
9. Eating in Holiness 32
10. Healing Insights 33
11. The Humility of Shabbat 35
12. The Teshuvah of Shabbat 37
13. Entering the Light 39
14. Connecting to the Tzaddikim 41
15. The Power of Song 46
16. Shabbat Talk 48
17. Eye to the Future 51
18. The Tzaddik is Called "Shabbat" 52
19. Clothes from the Garden of Eden 53
20. Eradicating Pride 56
21. Glimpse of the World to Come 58
22. The Compassion of Shabbat 60
23. Spending Shabbat with the Tzaddikim 62

Rosh Chodesh *The New Moon* 63
24. Days of Teshuvah 64
25. Even God Repents 65

Elul *Preparing for the Days of Awe* 69
26. A New Start 70
27. Teshuvah After Teshuvah 74
28. When One Plus One Equals One 77

Tishrei and Nisan 81
29. Two Seasons of Teshuvah 82

Rosh HaShanah ◾ *The New Year* ◾ 85
30 The Sound of the Shofar 86
31 The Shofar of Redemption 91
32 The Rosh HaShanah of the Tzaddik 94
33 Purifying the Mind 97
34 Overcoming Obstacles 99
35 Song of the Future 101
36 Healing the Eyes 104

Aseret Yemei Teshuvah ◾ *The Ten Days of Repentance* ◾ 109
37 "Seek God When He May Be Found" 110

Yom Kippur ◾ *Day of Atonement* ◾ 113
38 A Gift of Forgiveness 114
39 Reviving the "Dead Days" 117
40 Yom Kippur Paves the Way for Chanukah 120
41 Magnifying God's Name 121

Sukkot ◾ *The Festival of Booths* ◾ 125
42 In the Sukkah's Protective Shadow 126
43 Becoming One with God 127
44 "Sukkah-Consciousness" 130
45 Good Dreams 133
46 A Spiritual Harvest 134
47 Prayer for the Four Species 137
48 True Beauty 139

Hoshana Rabbah ◾ Shemini Atzeret ◾ Simchat Torah ◾ 141
49 When Heaven's Decree is Sealed 142
50 The Tikkun of Shemini Atzeret 145
51 The Unbroken Circle 147
52 Connecting Sukkot, Simchat Torah and Shavuot 149

Chanukah ◾ 151
53 Prayer Before Lighting the Menorah 152
54 Experiencing the World to Come in This World 154
55 Open Eyes 155
56 Igniting the Inner Flame 156
57 The Light of God's Face 157
58 Bringing Down the Light 158

Seventh of Adar ◾ *Yahrtzeit of Moses* ◾ 165
59 Searching for the Moses of Our Generation 166

Purim   173
60 Asking for Miracles 174
61 Banishing Haman, Crowning Mordekhai 185

Shalosh Regalim   *The Three Pilgrim Festivals*   187
62 Raising Up the Shekhinah 188
63 Seeing the Light of Yom Tov 191
64 "Serve God with Joy" 193
65 Eradicating the Three Cravings 196

Nisan   199
66 Magnetic Pull 200
67 Season of Our Liberation 206

Shabbat HaGadol   *The Shabbat Before Pesach*   209
68 Perceiving Divine Providence 210
69 Holy Fire 212

Pesach   219
70 Pesach Preparations 220
71 Purging the Heart of Chametz 221
72 Expanded Consciousness 224

Sefirat HaOmer   *Counting the Omer*   227
73 Entering the Gates of Holiness 228
74 Keys to the Royal Palace 230
75 Connecting Sefirat HaOmer to Purim 235

Lag BaOmer   *33rd Day of the Omer*   237
76 In the Merit of Rabbi Shimon bar Yochai 238

Shavuot   *The Festival of Weeks*   245
77 The Fiftieth Gate 246
78 Perfecting God's Kingship 248

Bein HaMetzarim   *The Three Weeks of Mourning Over Jerusalem*   251
79 Turning "Mourning" into "Morning" 252
80 Light Conquers Fire 257

Glossary   276

Appendix   *Selected Breslov Publications*   280

Preface

Chassidic thought distinguishes between *chitzoniyut* and *penimiyut*, the outer and inner dimensions. If we address only the outer aspect in our service of God, we may fulfill the strict requirements of the mitzvot but our spiritual life will lack vitality. Our sages tell us: "*Rachmana liba ba'ei* – The Merciful One desires the heart."[1] Going through the motions without feeling a connection to God not only makes for an incomplete service, but also an extremely dissatisfying one.

The distinction between *chitzoniyut* and *penimiyut* becomes even sharper on Shabbat and Yom Tov, days that are supposed to be "peak experiences" compared to the rest of the week and year. It is one thing to keep the laws of Shabbat, but quite another to experience the holiness and inner reality of Shabbat and make it our own.

"Shabbat is like a lavish wedding," Rebbe Nachman describes. "People are dancing and rejoicing with the greatest ecstasy. A man stands outside (looking in). He dresses himself in his best clothing and rushes to the wedding. He wishes to enter and join the festivities." But an outsider won't be able to blend into the festivities so easily just because he's wearing the right clothes. First he must work at preparing himself to understand and appreciate the joy and excitement that lie beyond his gaze. This is why Rebbe Nachman concludes his parable,

---

[1] *Sanhedrin* 106b; *Zohar* II, 162b; ibid., III, 281b; also cf. Rabbi Bachya Ibn Pakuda, *Chovot HaLevavot*, Introduction; Rabbi Yehudah HeChassid, *Sefer Chassidim*, 590.

ENTERING THE LIGHT

"One needs great merit even to look in through a tiny crack."[2]

How do we merit to glimpse the light and bask in the illumination of Shabbat and Yom Tov? Rebbe Nachman tells us: Pray for it!

Praying and longing create the "vessels" we need to enter the inner dimension of Shabbat and other holy days on the Jewish calendar. Reb Noson of Breslov, the foremost disciple of Rebbe Nachman, conveyed this idea to Reb Nachman of Tulchin, an orphan who grew up in his home, at the start of the Sukkot holiday one year. Reb Nachman had exerted himself to build the sukkah for Reb Noson's family, and at the end of the day was pleased with the result of his labors. Reb Noson told him, "You have done a fine job of building the sukkah. But do you know what it is to spend an entire afternoon yearning and praying to *experience* the sukkah?"[3] It is not enough merely to construct the "vessel" of a mitzvah; we must also seek its inner dimension.

At Rebbe Nachman's behest, Reb Noson took the lessons of *Likutey Moharan* and, one by one, turned them into prayers, until in the course of time he had composed an entire book of them called *Likutey Tefilot* (Collected Prayers). Reb Noson's prayers help us apply Rebbe Nachman's teachings to our own spiritual quest for holiness, personal refinement and, ultimately, knowledge of God.

Other prayers in this collection were taken from the writings of Reb Noson's disciple, Rabbi Nachman

---

[2] *Sichot HaRan* 254.
[3] Rabbi Shmuel Horowitz, *Avenehah Barzel*, 12.

PREFACE

Goldstein, best known as the Rav of Tcherin, a prolific author and outstanding thinker of the third generation of Breslover Chassidut. His *Tefilot VeTachanunim* (Prayers and Supplications) is actually an extension of *Likutey Tefilot*, elucidating certain points from the same lessons in *Likutey Moharan* that Reb Noson does not mention in his prayers. Several other prayers were penned by another close disciple of Reb Noson, Reb Ephraim ben Naftali, and published as *Tefilot HaBoker* (Prayers of the Dawn).

* * *

These prayers were translated from the original Hebrew into English with every attempt to preserve the author's tone and intention. Some selections did require minor adaptations, such as the rendering of grammatical constructions that do not read well in English, or the presentation of multiple scriptural verses which, in translation, detract from the personal tone of the prayers. Sometimes prayers turn on a dime from first-person singular to first-person plural. Therefore we occasionally changed the singular to plural or vice versa for the sake of consistency. In a few cases, we chose to abridge or modify certain passages in order to simplify a lengthy or complex prayer.

For readers who wish to explore Reb Noson's many scriptural, rabbinic and liturgical citations, we have provided appropriate references, along with brief explanations of technical concepts.

I am deeply grateful to Rabbi Chaim Kramer of Breslov Research Institute for the privilege of working on this project, and to our editor, Y. Hall, for the eloquent introductions to each prayer.

Readers will notice that certain ideas are repeated in these prayers. These occasional repetitions will always seem fresh and stimulating if the prayers are used for their primary purpose – as spiritual preparation for Shabbat and Yom Tov. Although Reb Noson was undeniably a poetic soul, this is not a book of poetry. It is a raft made of words to sail across the waters of our everyday struggles and concerns to these "islands in time," allowing us to experience the unique, rarefied atmosphere of Shabbat and Yom Tov to their fullest.

Here are keys forged by a master locksmith to unlock the closed doors of Shabbat and Yom Tov. May all who seek to enter the King's palace use them, and find their way inside.

Dovid Sears
Rosh Chodesh Adar 5767/2007
Yahrtzeit of my father and teacher,
Leib ben Yitzchak Yaakov, of blessed memory

Shabbat

1

Receiving Shabbat with Joy

Sunset approaches, the Shabbat candles are lit ... but are we truly ready to embrace this holy day? With this prayer we acknowledge how far we are from experiencing Shabbat – and how close we want to be.

May it be Your will, O God, that I receive the holy Shabbat with great joy and gladness, "with happiness, song, celebration and delight."[1] Protect me and save me so that no sadness or sorrow should arise in my heart, nor should I sigh or groan or worry about anything on the holy Shabbat. Rather, may I rejoice with all my strength, "with all my heart, and with all my soul, and with all my might,"[2] with boundless and endless joy, as truly befits the holy and awesome day of Shabbat. For on Shabbat, great joy and gladness without measure is awakened and reverberates through all the worlds.

Master of the Universe! What can I say, and what could I possibly say? I know too well how far I am from all this. As great and lofty as each mitzvah and holy trait surely is, and as beneficial as each mitzvah is for one who seeks holiness, that is how far I am from it – as far as one can be! This is especially true of the joy of Shabbat, upon which everything depends, since this joy enables us to come closer to You.

Yet You know how many obstacles we face, and what opposition is constantly arrayed against us to prevent us from experiencing the joy of Shabbat. Have mercy on me, O Merciful Father, and gladden me with Your deliverance constantly. Help me, save me and allow me to rejoice with the greatest ecstasy on every Shabbat, without exception. May I rejoice all day long on Shabbat, from its arrival until its departure, until I infuse even the six weekdays with the joy of Shabbat. So may I rejoice all week long, with true joy!

"My eyes shall see, and my heart shall rejoice, and my soul shall delight in Your deliverance!"[3]

(LT II, 13)

Notes
1. Liturgy, *Sheva Berakhot*.
2. Deuteronomy 6:5.
3. Liturgy, paraphrase of Evening Prayers.

2

Spiritual Exodus

The transition from the weekday to Shabbat can be compared to the transition from exile to redemption.

Master of the Universe! Mighty and Awesome One! Help me to attain "exalted fear," which is awe before Your Presence. This holy awe, combined with higher consciousness, comes from the joy of Shabbat.

O God full of mercy, Redeemer and Savior, Deliverer and Rescuer, save me, rescue me, and bring me forth from slavery to freedom, from exile to redemption! Enable me to rejoice on the holy Shabbat, so that I may greet Shabbat in a happy state of mind, "with wealth and honor, and with few mistakes."[1]

Help me to honor Shabbat with all my might, with every sort of gladness and joy and with every kind of pleasure and delight: to serve many delicious foods and drinks, and to wear the finest clothes in honor of Shabbat. But mainly I ask to be privileged to rejoice with all my heart on Shabbat with true joy and gladness, until through joy I go forth from slavery to freedom, from servitude to redemption.

Through the joy and freedom of Shabbat, may I attain sublime knowledge to the ultimate degree, as You truly desire. Thus may I experience true awe before You – holy awe combined with higher consciousness, without any trace of folly.

(LT II, 13)

Notes
1 Paraphrase of prayer recited by some after *Shalom Aleikhem*.

3

The Shabbat State of Mind

More than a day of physical delights, Shabbat is a portal to spiritual contentment and rejoicing in God.

Master of the Universe, All-Merciful One, Who is good and treats all creatures with goodness! Enable me to truly taste the sweetness of Shabbat. Grant me the joy and freedom of the holy Shabbat, and nullify the servitude of the six days of the week. Help me to cultivate a calm, settled mind, without conflict or agitation. May no thought of weekday pursuits, whether concerning business or any mundane activity, enter my mind on this holy day, and may my mind be entirely free from worry and oppressive thoughts. Rather, may it appear to me that all my work has been finished. So may I truly attain the peacefulness, rest, delight and joy of the holy Shabbat: "a rest of love and generosity, a rest of truth and faith, a rest of peace and serenity, tranquility and security – a perfect rest in which You find favor."[1]

"Gladden the soul of Your servant, for unto You, O God, I lift my soul."[2] In Your abundant mercy, enable me to rejoice constantly, especially on Shabbat and holy days. "Cause me to hear happiness and joy; may the bones that You crushed exult!"[3] For no one is capable of gladdening my soul but You alone, in Your immeasurable kindness alone, through Your hidden store of mercy alone. In the merit and power of the true tzaddikim, whom the *Zohar* calls "Shabbat of all the days,"[4] "satisfy us with Your goodness, cause our souls to rejoice in Your deliverance, and purify our hearts to serve You in truth."[5]

(LT II, 13)

Notes

1 Liturgy, Shabbat afternoon *Shemoneh Esrei*.
2 Psalms 86:4.
3 Psalms 51:10.
4 *Zohar* III, 144b.
5 Liturgy, Shabbat *Shemoneh Esrei*.

4

Getting Ready for Shabbat

A man's physical preparations on Friday afternoon include immersing in the mikveh and reviewing the weekly Torah portion with the Aramaic commentary of Onkelos. His spiritual preparations should include praying for the successful fulfillment of these mitzvot, with the ultimate goal of spiritual unification with God.

God of mercy, God of favor and goodwill! In Your great compassion and kindness, allow me to receive Shabbat with joy and gladness, with awe and love. Grant me the privilege of exerting myself physically in preparing for Shabbat, energetically and with the greatest enthusiasm.

Help me to always finish the weekly Torah portion with the congregation, reciting the weekly Torah portion twice in Hebrew and once in Aramaic with concentration, in holiness and purity. Thus may I perfect the Holy Tongue by restoring Aramaic to its source in Hebrew, which is the root and essence of all languages.[1]

Draw upon us the holiness of Shabbat when we bathe in hot water and immerse in the mikveh on Erev Shabbat. Help me, so that I never fail to bathe and immerse in honor of Shabbat. Just as I immerse myself in this world, so may You purify and sanctify my body, and sanctify my *nefesh*, *ru'ach* and *neshamah* in the supernal worlds. Send forth flames of Divine Fire from the fire of holiness above, which consumes and burns up all other fires. In this way, may You destroy and remove from me – as well as from the entire House of Israel – all mixtures of evil that cleave to us as a result of the Tree of Knowledge of Good and Evil, coupled with our own transgressions and wrongdoings. Thus the evil that cleaves to us will burn, fall away and disintegrate, and the good will be extricated and elevated and merge into the supernal goodness – into Your great goodness, which is eternal goodness. For this subjugation of evil and elevation of the good within us is an aspect of the perfection of the Holy Tongue, which is accomplished when we read the weekly Torah portion together with its Aramaic translation.

May we attain *Kedushat HaBrit* (Sanctification of the Covenant)[2] in truth, and return to You in truth. May we constantly progress from level to level in great holiness, according to Your beneficent will, until we reach and become subsumed within the Supernal Shabbat, the "day that is entirely Shabbat and contentment for the eternal life."[3]

(LT I, 19)

Notes

1 See Rashi on Genesis 2:23.
2 Sanctification of the Covenant refers to sexual purity – namely, adherence to the Torah's laws concerning marital relations. Ultimately, a person can transmute these energies to the spiritual goal of unification with God through *deveykut* and prayer. This process is discussed in *Likutey Moharan* I, 19, the lesson on which this prayer is based; also see ibid., I, 75 (end): "One must speak words of Torah and prayer until the body [i.e., one's physical nature] becomes utterly nullified. This is the paradigm of the verse, 'And they [Adam and Eve] became one flesh' (Genesis 2:24) – the body should become one with speech ... through Torah and prayer."
3 *Tamid* 7:4, cited in Shabbat morning service, *Ein K'Elokeinu*.

5

Extending Shabbat

The light of Shabbat shines far beyond temporal boundaries, illuminating each of the Four Worlds which God created – Atzilut (Emanation), Beri'ah (Creation), Yetzirah (Formation) and Asiyah (Action). By prolonging our experience of Shabbat each week, we draw its vitality and strength into our world, which is part of Asiyah.

God, have mercy and pour forth Your compassion upon me, for You know how far I am from the holiness of Shabbat. Grant me an undeserved gift, and impart the holiness of Shabbat to me.

May I add to the holiness of Shabbat before it arrives by refraining from forbidden labor well before sundown, and extend its holiness at its departure by refraining from forbidden labor until well after nightfall.[1]

Help me to infuse the weekdays with the sanctity of Shabbat, until all six days of mundane work become permeated with the holiness of Shabbat and are reabsorbed in their source, which is the holy Shabbat. Shabbat enlivens and sustains all six days of the week, along with all emanations, all creations, all formed things and all that is made, as well as all the worlds, from the very beginning point of Creation to the lowest point of the physical world. All their vitality and endurance derives from the holy Shabbat.

Master of the Universe! In Your great mercy, You gave us a beneficent gift, which You "kept hidden away in Your treasure trove, and 'Shabbat' is its name."[2] Therefore I have come to cast my prayer, my supplication and my request before You, O God and God of my fathers. Just as Your attributes of mercy and kindness overpowered Your attribute of strict justice so that You could confer upon us this holy gift, so may You pour forth Your beneficence from Your holy dwelling place and instill in us the ability to receive it. May we greet Shabbat with great holiness and with a joyous heart.

(LT I, 19)

Notes

1 According to the Torah, the restrictions of Shabbat and Yom Tov begin at nightfall and end at nightfall. However, the Talmudic sages created a "fence" by extending the commencement of these restrictions to a few minutes prior to sunset the day before, and lengthening their conclusion until the appearance of three medium-sized stars the night after. These laws are presented in *Shulchan Arukh, Orach Chaim* 260-261, and 293.

2 *Shabbat* 10b.

6

Shabbat Peace

The prophet Isaiah envisioned the ultimate peace of the future, when "the wolf shall lie down with the lamb and the leopard with the kid" (Isaiah 11:6). As Shabbat, the day of peace, approaches, we ask God to fill every aspect of our lives with peace.

May we sing and play music in praise of God constantly, until we become a channel for the melody that transcends all melodies, the "Song of Songs" of King Solomon, that man of peace whose very name means "peace." May we awaken all Ten Types of Melody that are expressed by the Book of Psalms,[1] and receive Your blessings of peace.

Bring peace to Your people, Israel – peace between friends and neighbors, peace between every husband and wife. May we never know hatred or jealousy, rivalry or strife. May this blessing of peace increase and spread to include all humanity, until everyone is able to rouse his fellow to seek the truth, to contemplate the ultimate purpose of Creation, and not waste his days on empty and meaningless pursuits. Then everyone will cast away the "false gods of silver and gold" and serve You in truth, with love and awe.

May we receive the peace of Shabbat with profound joy and gladness, and may You spread over us Your tent of peace. May we experience peace in our bodies, sparing us from any form of sickness or disease; and peace in our possessions, freeing us of greed and dishonest behavior, and let us not be harmed by the dishonesty of others in financial matters.

Grant us peace in our Torah studies, so that we may understand the words of Your Torah without confusion or difficulty, and receive new insights constantly, without any admixture of falsehood.

Bless us with peace, O God Who is exalted above all, and fulfill in us the prophecy of peace: "For in gladness you will go out, and in peace you will arrive; the mountains and the hills will burst into song before you, and all trees of the field will clap hands!"[2] "May the One Who makes peace in His heavens bring peace to us and to all Israel. Amen."[3]

(LT I, 27)

Notes

1 The Ten Types of Song are the "infrastructure" of the Book of Psalms, as discussed in *Pesachim* 117a and *Zohar* III, 101a. According to Rebbe Nachman, the Ten Types of Song are: *Berakhah, Ashrei, Maskil, Shir, Nitzu'ach, Nigun, Tefilah, Hodu, Mizmor* and *Hallelu-Yah* (*Likutey Moharan* II, 92).

2 Isaiah 55:12.

3 Liturgy, *Kaddish*.

7

The Secret of Faith

Rebbe Nachman teaches that by verbally declaring our faith, we strengthen our faith (see Likutey Moharan II, 44).

"Of God's kindness, forever I will sing; I will make known Your faithfulness from generation to generation with my mouth."[1]

I believe with complete faith in Your absolute Oneness, and in the renewal of the universe, and in Your true tzaddikim, and in Your holy Torah, both the Written Torah and the Oral Torah, as well as all the books of the true tzaddikim, and in the unity of Your people, Israel, whom You have chosen. For You are the Lord, God, in heaven, on earth and in the supernal worlds. "It is true that You are first and You are last, and apart from You there is no divinity."[2] You created heaven and earth and all their hosts, as well as Adam, the first man, during the six days of Creation, and on the seventh day You rested.

In Your love, O God, and in Your great mercy toward Israel, Your people, You gave us Your day of rest as an inheritance:

- a day of peace and holiness;
- a great, holy and awesome day;
- a day of cessation, rest and solace for the body and the soul, physically and spiritually, in this world and in all the worlds;
- a day when all worlds ascend from level to level, to the highest transcendent plane, to *Ra'ava DeRa'avin*, the sublime Will of Wills;

- a day entirely free from harsh judgment, entirely free from the Other Side and the kelipot;
- "a day that is entirely Shabbat," together with goodness, favor, love, kindness and absolute mercy;
- a day so holy and awesome that through it we may cleave to You and re-enter Your Oneness, and draw into our hearts perfect faith to carry us through the six days of the coming week.

Therefore I have come before You, O God and God of my fathers, God of Abraham, Isaac and Jacob, exalted God, Who is kind and beneficent. Be gracious to me in Your true kindness and abundant mercy, and give me the strength to receive Shabbat with great sanctity, joy and gladness, as befits every Jew. May I rejoice, delight and celebrate with all my might on this great, holy and awesome day. This is Shabbat:

- a day of joy and gladness throughout all the worlds;
- a day of delight for the Supernal King and Queen[3];
- a day that is entirely devoid of sadness, sighing and groaning;
- a day when even those condemned to Gehinnom may rest;
- a day full of radiance and goodness;
- a day when the Supernal Light shines throughout all the worlds – the "Light of the Living King's Face"[4];
- a day when holy and awesome "additional souls" (increased capacities for spiritual perception) are imbued within every member of Your people, Israel.

Our Father, our King, our Mighty One, our Creator, our Redeemer, our Holy One, Holy One of Jacob! Sanctify us with the holiness of Shabbat constantly, and help us to receive Shabbat in a befitting manner.

May we honor and enhance the delight of Shabbat with every sort of honor and delight, with food, drink and all kinds of delicacies, and may we not worry in the least about the expenses of Shabbat and Yom Tov, but trust in You, knowing that You will compensate us for all that we spend in honor of these holy days.[5] May we be blessed with fine and honorable clothes, and have many garments with which to honor Shabbat – fine, clean, holy and pure garments. Grant us pleasant dwellings in which to honor Shabbat, and may we light many candles on the eve of this holy day.

Protect us from the thirty-nine forbidden labors and their derivatives,[6] and prevent us from violating any law of Shabbat, whether scriptural or rabbinic. Help us to sanctify our mouths and our speech on Shabbat, so that we refrain from speaking about mundane matters that are not in keeping with the spirit of this holy day.

Master of the Universe, enable me to give tzedakah with an open hand to deserving people in need, in fulfillment of the verse: "He disbursed widely to the destitute; his righteousness endures forever."[7] May I be privileged to give the tzedakah of Shabbat by providing worthy poor people with Shabbat necessities, and by inviting worthy guests to my table every Shabbat.

May my heart be filled with the spirit of Shabbat constantly. Thus may I attain perfect faith: to believe and trust in You always, and to distribute tzedakah generously, with a good and joyous heart. May my tzedakah find favor in Your sight, through the faith with which I have been graced – for faith is the very essence and perfection of tzedakah and of the entire Torah. May the verse be established in me: "And he believed in God, and He accounted it for him as tzedakah."[8]

May the light of my tzedakah shine brightly by virtue of the holy Shabbat, in fulfillment of the verse: "And for you who fear My Name, a sun of tzedakah shall shine, with healing in her wings."[9]

Confer upon us blessing from the source of blessings – the blessing that issues forth from holy faith, which the holy Shabbat transmits to the six days of the week – for Shabbat is the source of blessing.

(LT I, 31)

Notes

1. Psalms 89:2.
2. Liturgy.
3. Kabbalistic euphemisms for God and the Shekhinah, corresponding to the sefirot of Tiferet and Malkhut.
4. Proverbs 16:15.
5. *Beitzah* 16a.
6. The Talmud enumerates thirty-nine categories of forbidden labors, derived from the work required for the construction of the Tabernacle in the desert; see *Shabbat* 7:2. In addition, the rabbis forbade certain derivatives of these constructive labors.
7. Psalms 112:9.
8. Genesis 15:6.
9. Malachi 3:20.

8

The Day That is Entirely Shabbat

Desire was given to man not to crave money and possessions, but to yearn for God and Godliness.

May we greet Shabbat with great joy and gladness, with song, praise, thanksgiving and melody, with "mirth, glad song, pleasure and delight," as when we dance before a bride and groom.

With the power of the holy Shabbat, may we destroy and eradicate the desire for wealth in our hearts, so that we feel no lust or attraction for money at all. Rather, may we constantly desire and yearn for the ultimate goal: the "day that is entirely Shabbat and contentment for the eternal life."[1]

(LT I, 49)

Notes
1 *Tamid* 7:4, cited in Shabbat morning service, *Ein K'Elokeinu*.

9

Eating in Holiness

Rebbe Nachman teaches that eating on Shabbat is not like eating during the six days of the week. While weekday eating provides physical gratification, Shabbat eating opens channels of blessing for the entire week (Likutey Moharan I, 276).

O God and God of our fathers, help me to attain the delight of Shabbat, to delight in God on the holy Shabbat, and to enhance the pleasantness of Shabbat with all sorts of delicacies, in holiness and purity and great joy. May I never be frugal in spending money for the sake of Shabbat or Yom Tov.

"You set a table before me, in view of those who afflict me; You anointed my head with oil; my cup overflows."[1] Be gracious to me in Your great mercy, and enable me to eat in holiness. May my meals always be conducted in the holiness that is drawn from the delight of Shabbat. Thus I will overcome all my inner spiritual adversaries and enemies, which are the ego and the tendency to lose touch with God, and "silence the foe and avenger."[2] All who rise up against me to do harm shall collapse and fall; their advice shall come to naught, and their evil designs shall be speedily foiled.[3]

(LT I, 57)

Notes

1. Psalms 23:5.
2. Psalms 8:3.
3. Liturgy, paraphrase of *Aleinu*.

10

Healing Insights

In the two loaves which we bless at the start of each Shabbat meal, Reb Noson finds an allusion to the double portion of Torah insights that we seek on this holy day.

May we bring forth new Torah insights on Shabbat, according to the paradigm of the holy *Zohar* that "two provide for one" – that is, the higher sefirot of Chokhmah and Binah transfer bounty to Z'er Anpin.[1] For true and holy Torah insights are a source of gratification and favor before You.[2]

May we draw forth *lechem mishneh* (double loaves) on Shabbat, which are *mishneh Torah* (double portions of Torah) that endow us with ever higher levels of perception. In Your mercy, grant us a double portion of *shefa*, the additional influx of Godliness which is *mishneh Torah*, on the holy Shabbat; and through Shabbat, may *shefa* flow to all worlds and all beings.

Help us to receive Shabbat with great joy, with awe and love and holiness and purity, and make Shabbat delightful in every way. Through the holiness of Shabbat, may we draw forth healing of body and soul. "Heal us from all disease and sickness and bring a complete cure to all our afflictions" – for You know our sickness of body and soul. "Heal us, O Lord, and we shall be healed, save us and we shall be saved, for You are our praise."[3]

Through the holiness of Shabbat, confer upon us an illumination of *teshuvah ila'ah* (the higher level of repentance),[4] and we will immediately return to You in truth. Inspire us to return to You out of love, according to Your beneficent will.

Draw forth grace, kindness, radiance, splendor and beauty upon all devout people of the generation, and may they find favor in the eyes of all who behold them. Heal them from all sickness and disease, and may all creatures gaze upon them with admiration.

May each one, according to his spiritual attainments, receive beauty, splendor and greatness in the eyes of all. May they become vessels to contain the "double portion" of Torah – new Torah insights – and on Shabbat, may they bring forth Torah insights without end.

(LT I, 58)

Notes

1. *Zohar* I, 32b, cited in *Likutey Moharan* I, 58. The ARI describes the process by which God sends an influx of *shefa* into this world via the network of the sefirot: *Abba* (Father), which is the *partzuf* (persona) of Chokhmah, transmits *shefa* to *Ima* (Mother), which is the *partzuf* of Binah. *Ima* then transmits it to Z'er Anpin, which is the *partzuf* of Tiferet. To receive *shefa*, Z'er Anpin ascends between *Abba* and *Ima*. In the *Zohar's* cryptic phrase, these are the "two that provide for one."
2. Reb Noson uses the common rabbinic phrase "before You" because God is ultimately beyond gratification. It is axiomatic that God is sufficient unto Himself; see Rabbi Aryeh Kaplan, *Handbook of Jewish Thought*, Vol. I, 3:35.
3. Liturgy, *Shemoneh Esrei*.
4. The Talmudic sages distinguish between repentance inspired by fear and repentance inspired by love. The latter is the higher level; see *Yoma* 86b.

11

The Humility of Shabbat

Gossip, slander and deceitful speech drive the Shekhinah into exile and rob us of closeness to God. Through humility, we regain what we have lost.

Merciful One, protect us from self-importance. May we always sense our essential humility in every limb of our bodies. Grace us with knowledge, understanding and insight so that we may follow the ways of humility without foolishness or self-deception, until we attain perfect humility in truth.

Save us in Your abundant mercy, and help us to guard our tongues against evil speech [slander] and gossip as well as all types of damaged speech [falsehood, profanity, flattery, etc.]. May not one bad word against any fellow Jew ever escape our lips, or any other form of damaged speech.

"My God, withhold my tongue from evil and my lips from uttering deceit."[1] Come to our aid, and do not allow us to be harmed by the damaged speech and evil speech of others. Do not let us be trapped by their arrogance through the sin of their mouths, God forbid. From now on, help us to guard against damaged speech, and may we sanctify our mouths always.

Protect us from all forms of arrogance and egotism. Elevate the Shekhinah from her exile, which was brought about by self-importance arising from the sin of evil speech. Deliver us from the grievous sin of evil speech, and enable us to sanctify the speech of our mouths with every type of holiness.

May we fully receive the radiance of Shabbat from the true sages of the generation. Redeem us from haughtiness, pride and conceit, and instill in us genuine humility. Then we will attain true life, holy life, complete healing of body and soul, and complete teshuvah motivated by love, all of which are drawn from the holy Shabbat.

Satiate us with Your goodness and grant us a taste of the holiness of Shabbat which enlivens all worlds, as it states, "Those who taste [Shabbat] merit life."[2] Confer upon us long life and a good life, a God-fearing life, a life in which we repudiate evil completely. May we return to You in truth and serve You in truth, with a whole heart and true humility all our days – both ourselves and our children, now and forever, until we attain "the day that is entirely Shabbat and contentment for the eternal life."[3] Amen.

(LT I, 58)

Notes
1   Liturgy, prayer after *Shemoneh Esrei*.
2   Liturgy, Shabbat *Musaf*.
3   *Tamid* 7:4, cited in Shabbat morning service, *Ein K'Elokeinu*.

12

The Teshuvah of Shabbat

The word ShaBbat is related to the word ShuV (return), which in turn is the root for the word TeShuVah (repentance). On Shabbat, explains the Baal Shem Tov, all things return to their Source, which is God.

Master of the Universe, Who performs wonders for the living: Act wondrously for me, so that I should not be considered dead while still alive.[1] Do what only You can do, so that I may achieve true teshuvah – the teshuvah of the holy Shabbat. May I commit myself resolutely to Torah study and Divine service, spending all my days in teshuvah with great devotion. And may I constantly be absorbed in the holiness of Shabbat, even during the six days of the week.

Through the holiness of Shabbat, may my eyes be opened so that I perceive my truly humble station. Grant me true humility. Let me think of myself as occupying a rung even lower than the extremely low rung upon which I stand; at least, may I never act as if I occupy a level that I have not reached, or stray beyond my proper bounds. May I know my place, which is too base and inferior to be measured or described, and may I harbor no hidden pride in my heart. Deliver me from all feelings of self-importance.

Father in Heaven, grant me the eyes of Shabbat, so that I will recognize my own lowliness in truth. I find myself beset by self-serving and prideful thoughts without number, and do not know any of the ways of true humility.

ENTERING THE LIGHT

O God, You know my heart! "You know my disgrace, my shame and my humiliation; all those who afflict me are before You."[2] Bring me back in perfect teshuvah. Deliver me from self-importance and the deceptions of the ego. Instill in me true humility to the point that I grasp my essential nothingness. Let me perceive the greatness and worthiness of Israel, Your holy nation, and may I sacrifice myself for it constantly.

(LT I, 81)

Notes

1. Reb Noson alludes to *Berakhot* 18b: "The wicked in their lifetime are called 'dead,' as it is written: 'And you, O wicked one, that is slain, the prince of Israel' (Ezekiel 21:30). And: 'At the mouth of two witnesses shall the dead be put to death' (Deuteronomy 17:6). He is still alive! However, he is already counted as dead."
2. Psalms 69:20.

13

Entering the Light

Each preparation we take to welcome Shabbat serves to banish each manifestation of the Other Side, clearing the way for our entry into the Infinite Light.

Every week, may I prepare for Shabbat with the greatest holiness, with love and desire, and with a heart full of joy and gladness. Help me so that no thought of worry or sorrow enters my mind, but let me rejoice with all my might on Shabbat, from beginning to end.

May I fulfill the mitzvah of bathing in hot water and cutting my fingernails every Erev Shabbat, as is proper, so that I banish and nullify all three completely impure kelipot, preventing them from having any attachment to me. In addition, may I extricate the good from the fourth kelipah, *nogah*, the "glowing husk," which is a mixture of good and evil surrounding the realm of holiness. Then all kelipot will fall to the depths and disappear, having no further grasp on the holy.[1]

Grant me the alacrity to extend Shabbat by accepting its sanctity before dusk, and not at the last minute; and instill in me the "additional soul" in purity and holiness every Shabbat. Together with the rest of the Jewish people who perform Your mitzvot with devotion, may I contribute to elevating all the worlds higher and higher, to the level called *Ra'ava DeRa'avin* (Will of Wills), until we merge into Your supernal holiness and enter the Infinite Light, according to Your beneficent will.

(LT I, 96)

■ ENTERING THE LIGHT

Notes

1 See *Zohar* II, 136b; Rabbi Chaim Vital, *Pri Etz Chaim, Sha'ar HaShabbat*, chap. 4; *Sha'ar HaKavanot*, pp. 62a-b; ibid., 62d. Rebbe Nachman mentions these preparations in *Likutey Moharan* I, 19:5.

14

Connecting to the Tzaddikim

Shabbat eating expands the influence of the true tzaddikim, whose teachings pave straight paths to God-consciousness and righteous living.

Help me to receive Shabbat in a fitting manner, "with great joy, with wealth and honor, and with few mistakes."[1] May I eat many foods in honor of Shabbat, and not hesitate to spend money on Shabbat and Yom Tov expenses. Instead, may I strengthen myself to honor Shabbat with fine food and drink and all sorts of delicacies, and may I eat heartily, as the Torah enjoins us: "Eat today, for today is a Shabbat unto God."[2] Our sages also encourage us to eat heartily on Shabbat, for "eating on Shabbat is entirely Divine, entirely holy, and ascends to a completely different place than our eating during the week."[3] By eating on Shabbat, we also rectify the spiritual damage caused by our having profaned Shabbat.[4]

O God, You know how hard it is for a human being of flesh and blood to observe Shabbat perfectly, without transgressing any of its laws. Therefore enable us to eat more than usual on Shabbat, in order to fix the damage caused by our having desecrated Shabbat in the past.

Through the holiness of eating on Shabbat – in particular, the service of eating performed by the true tzaddikim – may we broaden and increase the holy paths that the true tzaddikim revealed in the world.

Master of the Universe, God of all true tzaddikim! You alone know what the great tzaddikim have accomplished and done in the world – all the holy and awesome spiritual pathways that they uncovered, excavated and innovated. With what mighty efforts they exerted themselves! How many burdens they shouldered beyond measure and number! How much suffering and privation they endured with unceasing self-sacrifice, until they uncovered wondrous, straight paths in the desolate wilderness where no paths had existed before, where no man had ventured before! How they sacrificed themselves to traverse these paths again and again in order to pave the way for others!

However, due to our many sins and the coarse materialism of this world and its evil desires – especially widespread strife, scorn, envy, lust and craving after honor – these paths are still hidden to most of the world. Even the rare few who seek God and His tzaddikim and strive to follow in their wondrous ways, find these paths hidden from them.

You know that the tzaddikim revealed such profound spiritual advice and countless strategies that anyone can use to find direction and wise counsel wherever he may stand. Indeed, there is no situation or hour or individual bereft of a paved path to come closer to You, according to the advice, conversations, lessons and hints that the tzaddikim revealed to us in their holy and awesome teachings. "How great are Your deeds, O God; exceedingly profound are Your designs"[5] – for You illuminated us in these generations with the light of the holy teachings which the tzaddikim revealed to us!

Nevertheless, the tzaddikim taught that it is extremely difficult to help a person who possesses free choice.[6] Accordingly, all their wondrous ways and advice still remain hidden and removed from our sight, and their astounding and expansive pathways remain narrow and truncated, due to our materialism, confusion and foolish ways of thinking, which we brought upon ourselves through our evil deeds.

Therefore I come before You, Master of Compassion, Guide of Penitents, and ask You to help me to receive Shabbat with the greatest holiness and joy, and to eat heartily on this holy day. In this way, I can expand and increase all the pathways of holiness that a person must follow in order to come close to You in truth.

Through the holiness of Shabbat, may we elevate the aspect of the "legs" (the lowest levels on the ladder of Creation) to the supernal realm of holiness, as it is written: "If you allow your foot to rest on Shabbat."[7] All the mitzvot we perform during the six days of the week will lift up their "feet" from the kelipot and the Other Side, which leech vitality from them during the weekdays, so that each mitzvah can "walk" and present itself before You.

In Your great compassion and love for Your people, Israel, please accept our mitzvot and good deeds – even those performed by people of low stature like myself, who serve You in a state of extremely constricted consciousness, entirely lacking wholeness. Accept them all lovingly and esteem them; take pride in them with the greatest delight. Like a father toward a little child, show us favor, and treasure and exaggerate the worth of our meager good deeds, which are so lacking in substance, quantity and quality. Your love and delight will become so great that the holy path created by our mitzvot will be widened and increased, in fulfillment of the verse: "Righteousness shall walk before Him, and set his footsteps on the path."[8] The footsteps of our mitzvot and good deeds will create a wide, paved path, and widen the awesome holy paths that our preeminent tzaddikim forged in this world.

Have mercy on the paths of the tzaddikim in the merit of the holy Shabbat meals, and widen and increase them. Reveal them to us and to Your entire nation, the House of Israel. Then we will walk in the holy ways of the tzaddikim in truth, and return to You in perfect repentance from all the evil places and paths to which we have strayed.

Have mercy on us and do not destroy us; have pity and compassion, and always lead us in Your holy paths, which You revealed through Your awesome tzaddikim. You alone know the awesome truth of their wondrous paths. "Lead me on the path of Your mitzvot, for that is my desire."[9] "Lead me in Your truth and teach me, for You are the God of my deliverance; for You I have hoped all the day."[10] "Teach me, O God, the way of Your statutes, and I will cherish it above all."[11] "Teach me, O God, Your way, that I may walk in Your truth; unite my heart to fear Your Name!"[12]

Come to my aid, Master of Deliverance! Save me from all dire straits! My needs are so many, and my mind is so constricted that I cannot put even an iota of them into words.

Rescue me from contention and strife. Grant me true peace within my heart and in my activities in the world. Instill in me true love of others. Allow me to go in the ways of the true tzaddikim, according to Your will and the will of those who truly fear You, now and forever. Let our portion be with them, and we will never be disgraced; for in You we place our trust, and we rely on Your great kindness in truth.

"May the One Who makes peace in His heavens bring peace to us and to all Israel. Amen."[13]

(LT I, 107)

Notes

1. Paraphrase of prayer recited by some after *Shalom Aleikhem*.
2. Exodus 16:25, referring to the manna from heaven.
3. *Likutey Moharan* I, 125; cf. ibid, 57:5.
4. *Likutey Moharan* I, 277.
5. Psalms 92:6.
6. *Chayey Moharan* 197.
7. Liturgy. Reb Noson alludes to the aspect of Malkhut, symbolized by the foot, the lowest limb of the body upon which the entire structure stands. Malkhut attains perfection through Shabbat.
8. Psalms 85:14.
9. Psalms 119:33.
10. Psalms 25:5.
11. Psalms 119:35.
12. Psalms 86:11.
13. Liturgy, *Kaddish*.

15

The Power of Song

Like a magnet to metal, song attracts and pulls the soul. On Shabbat we sing songs of joy and gladness to draw our hearts closer to God.

Master of the Universe, Who protects Israel forever! Protect me and save me from the sad songs that wicked people sing most of the time, and which the world finds so irresistible. You know how much harm these melodies cause, and how much damage they do to the Jewish people, who strive to live according to Your Torah. Have mercy on us in the merit of the true tzaddikim, and come to our aid constantly to save us from them.

Enable us to gladden our souls always, in holiness and purity, with joyous songs and melodies that draw our hearts to You and to Your service, Your Torah and Your tzaddikim. Strengthen us with the power of the true tzaddikim, so that we may elevate these songs of the wicked through the holiness of Shabbat. Give us the ability to transform them to joy when we sing them on Shabbat.

May the merit of the holy Shabbat shield us, so that these songs have no power to bring us to depression or grief. Rather, may we refine and elevate these songs, transforming them from sorrow and sighing to joy and gladness. In this way, may we come closer to You and be drawn after You, "rejoicing like a mighty warrior to run the course."[1] May we go in Your ways, engage in Your Torah and fulfill Your commandments – to cleave and bind ourselves to You and Your tzaddikim, in truth and faith, with a firm, unbreakable bond.

SHABBAT

May we sing many songs and melodies in praise of You on Shabbat and Yom Tov with the greatest happiness and delight, melodies of mirth and exultation without any trace of sadness, worry or downheartedness. "Satisfy us with Your goodness, cause our hearts to rejoice in Your deliverance, and purify our hearts to serve You in truth."[2]

(LT I, 138)

Notes
1 Psalms 19:6.
2 Liturgy, Shabbat *Shemoneh Esrei*.

16

Shabbat Talk

When we perfect our speech on Shabbat, we infuse the rest of the week with the same joy and tranquility that we experience on the holy day.

Have mercy on us for the sake of Your Name, and cause the truth to shine through the "square of speech," which represents the four aspects of speech,[1] until we attain the perfection of speech in truth. Help us to attain perfect speech, which is the perfection of the Holy Tongue, to the extent that we can transmit the holiness and joy of Shabbat to the six days of the week and rejoice constantly, even during the weekdays, in Your Name and Your service.

Let us receive Shabbat with great holiness, gladness, joy and a good heart. Do not allow any trace of anxiety or sadness to enter our hearts on the holy Shabbat, or any sort of grief; remove from us all sighs and groans. In Your favor, O Lord our God, create an atmosphere of tranquility for us, so that there will be "no suffering or sighing and groaning on our day of rest."[2] May we rejoice greatly on every Shabbat with true joy, with "gladness, song, happiness and mirth,"[3] according to Your beneficent will.

Let us transmit the holiness of Shabbat to the six days of the week, until we can rejoice on weekdays too, and always be happy. We will delight and rejoice in You constantly, and perform all the mitzvot with great joy, even during the six days of the week, and be thoroughly happy. In Your salvation we will delight and rejoice, as it is written: "Serve God with joy, come before Him with glad song! Know that the Lord is our God; He made us, and we belong to Him – His people, and the sheep of His pasture!"[4]

Enable us to constantly infuse the six days of the week with the joy of Shabbat – until the Simple Oneness that underlies the diversity of Creation becomes revealed throughout the world, and all beings know and believe that all multiplicity comes from the absolutely Simple Unity of God, may He be blessed and elevated forever and for all eternity. "And every created thing shall know that You created it, and every formed thing shall understand that You formed it; and everything that possesses the breath of life in its nostrils shall declare: 'The Lord, God of Israel, is King, and His dominion extends over all!'"[5]

Your Simple Oneness will be revealed to all humanity through Your people, Israel, whom You chose as a unique nation from all nations on the face of the earth. "For You are One, and Your Name is One, and who is like Your people, Israel, one nation on earth?"[6] After the Simple Oneness has been revealed through the multiplicity of this lower world, due to the efforts of Your holy people, Israel, the Simple Oneness will also be revealed above, throughout the supernal realms. All strife and conflict will be nullified, and great peace will be drawn into the world, all as a result of our rejoicing on Shabbat.

(LT II, 2)

Notes

1   The Kabbalists symbolized Shabbat as a circle with a square in the middle; see *Zohar* Introduction, 5b. In *Likutey Moharan* I, 59,

Rebbe Nachman relates the circle to the *Heikhal HaKodesh*, the Holy Chamber of souls surrounding the tzaddik, and the square to the tzaddik's attribute of judgment. The "fire" of this judgment purifies the souls of spiritual dross. Rebbe Nachman also relates the symbol of the square to the four aspects of speech in *Likutey Moharan* II, 2. Speech, like Shabbat, is associated with the sefirah of Malkhut.

2   Liturgy, Shabbat *Shemoneh Esrei*.
3   Paraphrase of *Sheva Berakhot*.
4   Psalms 100:2-3.
5   Liturgy, Rosh HaShanah *Musaf*.
6   Liturgy, Shabbat afternoon *Shemoneh Esrei*.

17

Eye to the Future

Shabbat affords us the opportunity to look beyond our physical existence to the ultimate purpose of Creation.

Help us to receive Shabbat properly, with great joy and gladness, and with wondrous *deveykut*, according to Your beneficent will. May we merit to know and grasp the ultimate purpose of heaven and earth, which is to know and perceive You through everything in the world, according to Your will and the will of those who truly revere You – until we attain the "day that is entirely Shabbat and contentment for the eternal life."[1]

(LT II, 28)

Notes

1 *Tamid* 7:4, cited in Shabbat morning service, *Ein K'Elokeinu*.

18

The Tzaddik is Called "Shabbat"

Having attained the highest levels of moral purity and spiritual insight, the tzaddik blazes a path that others may follow in their quest for Godliness.

Let us greet Shabbat in a joyous frame of mind, and strive with all our strength to make Shabbat a delight, rejoicing on each and every Shabbat with true joy.

Through our celebration of Shabbat, may we draw upon ourselves the holiness of the consciousness of the *Rosh Bayit*[1] – the tzaddik who stands at the very fountainhead of Creation, having reached the all-encompassing root of the Torah; the tzaddik whom the Zohar calls "Shabbat of all the days."[2]

May we return to You in truth and become subsumed within Your great Name, as our sages teach us: "Your Name is bound up with our names."[3] And may we fix all the spiritual damage we have caused to Your great Name.

(LT II, 33)

Notes

1. *Tikkuney Zohar, Tikkun* 3, 18a. Rebbe Nachman discusses this concept in *Likutey Moharan* II, 67.
2. *Zohar* III, 144b.
3. *Yerushalmi Ta'anit* 2; Rashi on Joshua 7:9; Rashi on Jeremiah 14:7; et al. Rebbe Nachman weaves this theme into his lesson in *Likutey Moharan* II, 66 and 67. In both cases, he relates the Divine Name to Shabbat.

19

Clothes from the Garden of Eden

The first man and woman whom God placed in the Garden of Eden were robed in "garments of light." That same spiritual clothing can be ours when we embrace the awesome holiness of Shabbat.

Grant us the holiness of Shabbat, and keep us far from all mundane labor. Free us from all weekday activities in order to engage in Torah study, prayer and Divine service, constantly, in truth. Let us be "free men" in truth!

Merciful One! You gave us this "precious gift which was stored away in Your treasure trove – 'Shabbat' is its name."[1] You know the great loftiness and preciousness of the holy Shabbat, which enlivens and sustains all the worlds. And You know how far I am from the holiness and joy of Shabbat.

Please, God, Who alone is Master over all Creation, Who is "good and does good to all,"[2] "great in counsel and great in deed"[3] – help me, save me, teach me and instruct me so that I may constantly attain the true joy of Shabbat and rejoice on each and every Shabbat. Allow me to experience the "taste" of the holy Shabbat!

May I always remember the holy Shabbat, as it is written: "Remember the Shabbat day, to sanctify it."[4] Confer upon me the holiness of Shabbat throughout the six days of the week, so that the ordinary weekdays become sanctified with the holiness of Shabbat; and through the holiness of Shabbat, may I be found worthy of receiving all blessings from their source above.

In the merit of Shabbat, may I speedily reach the true goal: to truly grasp the "ultimate knowledge, which is 'not-knowing'"[5] – to understand and perceive in truth that wisdom remains far from me. As it is written: "I said, 'I shall become wise,' but it is far from me."[6] May I merge into the paradigm of the "Place of the World,"[7] the ultimate reality that encompasses the entire universe, which was created with wisdom.[8]

In Your great compassion, help me to cast off this leprous body, which is the "skin of the serpent,"[9] and put on "Shabbat clothing," which is a holy spiritual body from the Garden of Eden!

(LT II, 42)

Notes

1. *Shabbat* 10a.
2. *Birkat HaMazon* (Grace After Meals).
3. Jeremiah 32:19.
4. Exodus 20:8.
5. *Likutey Moharan* I, 24:8; ibid., II, 7:6, 83, citing *Bechinat Olam* 13:13. There are levels upon levels of "not-knowing," as mentioned in *Chayey Moharan* 282, 283, et passim. Also see the well-known parable of the Baal Shem Tov cited by Rabbi Aharon of Zhelikhov, *Keter Shem Tov* 3, concerning two men who wish to see the king. One greatly exerts himself to search through all the chambers of the royal palace, beholding the many marvels therein, but in the end fails to achieve his purpose. The other fellow assumes he won't succeed, and therefore doesn't even try. Concerning this, God says, "Would that they had abandoned Me, but kept My Torah!" Meaning: If only they had given up after dedicating all their strength to explore the inner dimensions of Torah. This seems to be the precursor of Rebbe Nachman's teachings on knowing and not-knowing.

6   Ecclesiastes 7:23.
7   That is, God is the ultimate context of all creation and the Ultimate Reality. *Bereshit Rabbah,* 68:9, cited by Rashi on Exodus 33:21; cf. *Likutey Moharan* II, 1:14; ibid., II, 56.
8   Cf. Psalms 104:24.
9   *Zohar* II, 265a. Rebbe Nachman mentions this concept in *Likutey Moharan* II, 82, which is the basis for this prayer.

20

Eradicating Pride

Were we only to open our eyes, we would comprehend how truly small and insignificant we are, and how truly lofty and exalted is God.

Enable us to receive Shabbat in its totality, opening the Gates of Understanding for us so that we will be capable of contemplating Your loftiness and splendor. May we clearly recognize our lowly and humble station, and not be like those who "act like Zimri and seek the reward of Pinchas."[1] On the contrary, may we search our souls thoroughly and ask ourselves how can we occupy such a low and inferior rung, when in truth we should be on an extremely lofty level, as befits the Jewish people? Is this the purpose for which You formed us, and chose us from among all the nations? You called us by Your great and holy Name and performed so many kindnesses and wondrous miracles for us at every time and hour – yet in our folly we strayed after the advice of our evil inclination, until we fell to such a low and inferior place as this!

Open the "eyes of the mind" for us in the merit of the holiness of Shabbat, so that we may behold with lucid perception Your exaltedness and splendor, and by contrast, our profound lowliness and inferiority, until we attain true humility. May we be absolutely unimpressed with ourselves and recognize our place, not deluding ourselves with feelings of pride or arrogance. Thus may we come to revere Your great Name in truth, and be filled with awe before You at all times.

Instill in us perfect faith so that we may merit to witness the rebuilding of Jerusalem and the ingathering of the exiles. As it is written: "The builder of Jerusalem is God; the dispersed of Israel, He will gather in."[2] Amen – may this be Your will!

(*Tefilot VeTachanunim* II, *Tefilah* 14)

Notes
1. *Sotah* 22b. Meaning: One may not act like the wicked and expect the reward of the righteous.
2. Psalms 147:2.

21

Glimpse of the World to Come

Our sages teach that Shabbat is one-sixtieth of the World to Come. In this prayer we ask God to shine even more of the illumination of the World to Come upon us.

Master of the Universe! You have made known to us the loftiness and sanctity of Shabbat. By receiving this day with honor and holiness, as is fitting, may we be granted "open eyes" – eyes with which to perceive our lowliness and God's exaltedness.

Have mercy on us and enable us to fully receive the holiness of Shabbat, and save us from every sort of desecration of Shabbat, may the Merciful One protect us. May we truly be among those who "guard Shabbat and not desecrate it."[1] As our rabbis of blessed memory declared: "Whoever observes Shabbat according to its laws, all his sins will be pardoned – even if he served idols like the generation of Enosh."[2]

Through the holiness of Shabbat, may we attain true humility, nullifying self-importance and conceit to the ultimate degree. May we destroy and nullify all heresy, idolatry and damaged faith; may we believe in You with perfect faith. Then all harsh judgments will be removed from us and from the entire House of Israel.

Correct and fill the deficiency of the moon, which is bound up with Your attribute of Malkhut, and bring about a complete unification of the Divine Name *YHVH* and the Divine Name *Elokim*.[3] Fulfill the verse that states: "And God will be King over all the earth; on that day the Lord will be One and His Name will be One."[4] Draw upon us a complete and true illumination, an illumination of the World to Come; for then Your great Name *YHVH* will be pronounced the way it is written, as our rabbis of blessed memory declare.⁵

(*Tefilot VeTachanunim* II, *Tefilah* 10)

Notes

1   Isaiah 56:2.
2   *Shabbat* 118a.
3   The Kabbalists associate *YHVH*, God's Essential Name, with the sefirah of Tiferet, and *Elokim*, the name associated with God's rulership over all creation, with the sefirah of Gevurah (or, in some cases, Malkhut; e.g., see *Likutey Moharan* I, 4:2). Accordingly, the unification of these two Names variously represents the synthesis of the six days of the week (Tiferet) with Shabbat (Malkhut), the profane with the sacred, and the masculine/active with the feminine/receptive.
4   Zechariah 14:9.
5   *Pesachim* 50a.

22

The Compassion of Shabbat

Anger and cruelty ravage the world; a lack of compassion and caring cries out from every corner. If only we could master the attribute of compassion, God would show us more compassion, too.

"You graciously confer Divine knowledge upon man, and teach each person understanding. Grace us with wisdom, understanding and knowledge."[1] Then we may cleave to the Divine attribute of compassion, and acquire the ability to show compassion toward all creatures.

Save us from all forms of anger and cruelty, which result from foolishness and the absence of Divine knowledge. Rather, let us constantly strengthen and compel ourselves to be compassionate, and may You show compassion toward us from Heaven, as our sages taught: "Whoever shows compassion toward other creatures will be shown compassion from Heaven."[2]

Master of the Universe! You know how badly we need deliverance and mercy from Heaven, each person in his own way – for You alone know all the travail that everyone endures all the time, materially and spiritually. This particularly applies to the Jewish people, collectively and individually, so many of whom are impoverished, sick and weighted down with great suffering. You know how lacking we are in strength and knowledge, to the point that we are powerless to evoke Your mercy fully, as is needed – for mercy and compassion primarily depend on Divine knowledge.

However, You have made known to us that the holy Shabbat is an instrument of Divine knowledge. Shabbat transmits higher consciousness to every Jew. Therefore we beg You: Have mercy on us and grant us the privilege of receiving Shabbat in a proper manner. May we receive the light of Divine knowledge, and in so doing, attain the Divine attribute of compassion.

(*Tefilot VeTachanunim* I, *Tefilah* 14)

Notes
1 Liturgy, *Shemoneh Esrei*.
2 *Shabbat* 151b; *Bava Metzia* 85a; *Megillah* 12b; *Yerushalmi Bava Kama* 8:7; *Zohar* III, 92b; also see *Likutey Moharan* I, 119.

23

Spending Shabbat with the Tzaddikim

This prayer may refer to spending Shabbat with any true tzaddik; to spending Shabbat at the gravesites of holy tzaddikim such as the Baal Shem Tov in Medzibuzh, Rabbi Shimon bar Yochai in Meron, or the ARI in Tzefat; or to spending Shabbat at the gravesite of Rebbe Nachman in Uman.

Grant me the privilege of spending Shabbat frequently with the true tzaddikim, and sitting with them at their table on this holy day. You have taught us that just as fasting purifies the heart, so does spending Shabbat with a true Torah sage. May I come close to the true tzaddik who has attained the loftiest spiritual levels – for spending Shabbat with such a tzaddik will enhance my Divine service far more than many, many fast days![1]

(*Tefilot VeTachanunim* I, *Tefilah* 24)

Notes

1 *Likutey Moharan* I, 167.

Rosh Chodesh
The New Moon

24

Days of Teshuvah

The first day of every Hebrew month – known as Rosh Chodesh (Head of the Month) – is an auspicious time for breaking all barriers and returning to God wholeheartedly.

God of forgiveness and mercy, help us to return to You in perfect teshuvah. Do not let us depart from this world until we have repented for our sins. May we fix all the damage we have done before You in thought, speech and action.

Enable us to draw upon ourselves the light of teshuvah from its source, which is Rosh Chodesh, as You revealed to us through Your true tzaddikim.[1] Let us experience the essence of teshuvah on the first days of all twelve months of the year – these are the days of Rosh Chodesh, which You gave to the Jewish people as "a time of atonement throughout all their generations."[2] Then we will surely return to You in truth.

(LT I, 10)

Notes

1. *Likutey Moharan* I, 10:9.
2. Liturgy, Rosh Chodesh *Musaf*.

25

Even God Repents

This prayer by Rabbi Nachman Goldstein of Tcherin paraphrases the Rosh Chodesh Musaf Shemoneh Esrei and the ceremony of Kiddush Levanah (Sanctification of the New Moon), relating both to the theme of teshuvah.

"The days of Rosh Chodesh You gave to Your people as a time of atonement throughout all their generations."[1]

Master of the Universe! Grant us the privilege to raise all our children to follow the ways of Torah, to escort them to the *chupah* (marriage canopy) and to initiate them into the performance of good deeds. Spare us the many difficulties of child-rearing, and confer upon us and upon all our offspring a long and good life.

Master of the Universe! You have made known to us that the death of small children, may God spare us, is a result of the mystery of the diminution of the moon. This is why the word *me'orot* (luminaries) is written in the Torah deficiently, without the letter *vav* – and our sages explain that this alludes to infant mortality, God forbid.[2] Likewise, You have made known to us that Rosh Chodesh, when the moon begins to wax and thereby attain its tikkun, is "a time of atonement throughout all our generations." Due to Your "repentance," so to speak, for having diminished the moon, You instructed the Jewish people to bring the Additional Offerings of Rosh Chodesh as atonement on Your behalf.[3] Accordingly, on Rosh Chodesh, atonement, forgiveness and pardon are extended to all generations of Israel, who are compared to the moon,[4] and they are granted a long and good life.

Have mercy on us and enable us to receive the holiness of Rosh Chodesh in a fitting manner. "May it be Your will to bring us up in joy to our Land and to plant us within our borders. There we shall bring our obligatory offerings before You – the Daily Burnt Offerings according to their order and the Additional Offerings according to their rule; and we shall prepare and sacrifice the Additional Offerings of Rosh Chodesh before You in love, in accordance with the command of Your will. Thus You instructed us in Your Torah through Moses, Your servant, in Your glorious Name, as it states: "On your Rosh Chodesh days you shall sacrifice a Burnt Offering unto God: two young bullocks, one ram and seven yearling male sheep, without flaw; and their meal offerings. For Your nation, Israel, You have chosen from all the nations, and the statutes of Rosh Chodesh days, You have fixed for them."[5]

Master of the Universe! You have made known to us that when we recite the Torah passages that describe the sacrificial offerings, You consider it as if we had actually brought all the sacrifices at their proper times and in their proper places, according to their laws.[6] Therefore may it be Your will that when we recite the passage, "On your Rosh Chodesh days" – even if it is not Rosh Chodesh – You will consider it as if we had brought the Rosh Chodesh offering in its proper time. Confer upon us something of the tikkun and restoration of the moon, and grant atonement, forgiveness and pardon to all generations of Israel, that we receive a long and good life. May we fulfill the mitzvah of blessing the New Moon every month at the proper time.

Restore the moon's lost light, and may it be spared every aspect of smallness. "May the light of the moon be like the light of the sun, and the light of the sun like the light of the seven days of Creation, as was the case before it was diminished, as it is written: 'And God made the two great luminaries.'[7] Fulfill in us the verse: 'And they shall seek the Lord their God, and David their king.'[8] Amen!"[9]

(*Tefilot VeTachanunim* I, *Tefilah* 21)

Notes

1. Liturgy, Rosh Chodesh *Musaf*.
2. *Yerushalmi Ta'anit* 4:3. The omission of the letter *vav* renders the word *me'eirot*, "curses." The Talmudic sages understand the curse to be diphtheria, one of the prime causes of infant mortality. (It seems implicit in this interpretation that the moon symbolizes the feminine principle, so its diminution indicates a deficiency related to motherhood.)
3. See *Chulin* 60b.
4. Maharsha on *Chulin* 60b; see also *Likutey Halakhot, Tefilin* 5:19; *Rosh Chodesh* 4; *Eidut* 5:13, 14; *Nefilat Apayim* 4:20.
5. Liturgy, Rosh Chodesh *Musaf*.
6. *Menachot* 110a.
7. Genesis 1:16.
8. Hosea 3:5. King David is the personification of Malkhut, which is symbolized by the moon.
9. Liturgy, *Kiddush Levanah*; cf. Isaiah 30:26.

Elul

Preparing for the Days of Awe

26

A New Start

Based on the Kabbalistic meditations of the ARI for the month of Elul, this prayer expresses the idea that teshuvah means repudiating our misdeeds completely and making a new start.

O God and God of our fathers! Have mercy on me and on the miserable state of my soul, which thirsts and hungers and desires to truly return to You! In Your abundant mercy, help me to attain complete teshuvah for all my sins, transgressions and evil deeds, and to be included among those of whom it states: "Heaven helps whoever seeks purity."[1] Surely You will help me from Heaven to purify me of my sins and enable me to repent completely for all my transgressions.

God full of mercy! Please show me Your great compassion and behold my poverty and lowliness. For what purpose was I created, since right now I cannot be considered a creature at all? It is as if I never came into existence, for it would have been better for me had I not been created, since I have behaved wickedly.[2]

Therefore I come before You, O Lord my God, to invoke the power of Your great Name *EHYH*,[3] by which You were called when You began to redeem Your children from Egypt to make them Your nation. As You made known to Moses at the Burning Bush: "Thus you shall say to the Children of Israel: '*EHYH* has sent me to you!'"[4] In the power of this Divine Name, help me to prepare myself to exist in the world. Let me feel the pain of my many sins and transgressions, and return to You in wholehearted teshuvah.

May I be among those who are "disparaged, but do not disparage in return, who hear their disgrace, but do not respond."[5] "When others curse me, let my soul remain silent."[6] After all the forms of shame and insult that I may hear from people who denigrate me, may I remain silent and not respond in kind. As it is written: "Be silent before God, and hope unto Him."[7] May I be "like a man who does not hear, and in whose mouth there are no rebuttals"[8]; "like one who is deaf, and will not hear; like one who is mute, and will not open his mouth."[9]

O God, in truth I know that all the embarrassments in the world would not be enough for me because of the number and gravity of my sins. I am far more despicable than all this, more than the mouth can express – for due to my many sins I damaged Your glory, which is so vast and holy, and failed to honor Your great Name. I disgraced my own soul exceedingly through my misdeeds, and gave strength to the blood in the left ventricle of the heart, which is the physical seat of the evil inclination.[10] Surely it is incumbent upon me to suffer much shame and "bloodshed" – for when one blushes with embarrassment, it is counted as if his blood has been shed. Help me, God, never to respond to those who disgrace me, so that this may atone for all my transgressions.

O God, my soul knows too well how far I am from sincere teshuvah. My sins have gone over my head and my mind has become so confused that I no longer know how to return to You. My higher consciousness has departed from me and my heart has abandoned me. I wander in the world, lost and directionless, without intellect and without heart.

"O God, You know my folly, and my trespasses are not hidden from You."[11] Now, my Father, my Merciful Father, what can I do? To where can I flee for help? How can I find a healing balm, a plan and advice to save my life, to deliver my soul from destruction? "I raise my eyes to the mountains – from where will my help come?"[12]

Help me! Help me! Show Your grace to me! Save me in Your great mercy and kindness, and from Your holy dwelling bestow upon me a spirit of wisdom and understanding, a spirit of holiness and purity, so that I can truly become holy and pure, and return to You in perfect teshuvah!

May I remain absolutely silent before all those who scorn and embarrass me, in fulfillment of the verse: "Be silent before God, and hope unto Him."[13] Enable me to bear disgrace and shame and "bloodshed" for my sins, and to accept everything with love.[14]

(LT I, 6)

Notes

1 *Shabbat* 104a, et al.; cf. *Zohar* II, 79b, et passim.
2 See *Sanhedrin* 38a: "At the hour when the Holy One, blessed be He, sought to create man, He created one faction of ministering angels whom He asked, 'Is it your wish that I create man?' They replied, 'Master of the Universe, what will be the nature of his deeds?'"
3 Literally, "I will be."
4 Exodus 3:14.
5 Paraphrase of *Yoma* 23a: "Regarding those who are disparaged but do not disparage in return, who hear their disgrace but do not respond, who serve [God] with love and rejoice in suffering, it is written, 'Those who love [God] shall be like the sun when

it shines forth in its strength' (Judges 5:31)." Rebbe Nachman addresses the issue of equanimity in *Likutey Moharan* I, 4:1, 33:1, 65:3 and 251; *Sichot HaRan* 51; et passim. For teachings from the Baal Shem Tov on equanimity, see my anthology, *The Path of the Baal Shem Tov* (Jason Aronson, 1997), pp. 47-49.

6 Liturgy, paragraph after *Shemoneh Esrei*.
7 Psalms 37:7.
8 Psalms 38:15.
9 Psalms 38:14.
10 See Rabbi Shneur Zalman of Liadi, *Tanya*, Part I, ch. 9; Rabbi Chaim Vital, *Etz Chaim*, Part II, *Sha'ar Kitzur ABYA*, ch. 4 (115b).
11 Psalms 69:6.
12 Psalms 121:1.
13 Loc. cit.
14 The Talmudic sages extol the acceptance of afflictions with love; for example, "Whoever rejoices in the sufferings that befall him brings redemption to the world" (*Ta'anit* 8a). "The Torah is acquired through forty-eight qualities: acceptance of suffering" (*Avot* 6:5). Not only does suffering bring atonement, but it draws us nearer to God, when we accept the suffering humbly and do not question God's justice. Rabbi Klonymus Kalman Shapira of Piaseczna discusses the spiritual mechanics of this issue in *Derekh HaMelekh, Chayei Sarah, Ma'amar* 1.

27

Teshuvah After Teshuvah

Repentance is an ongoing process in which we ask forgiveness not only for our misdeeds, but also for our previously limited perception of God's greatness. Accordingly, Rebbe Nachman teaches, even a tzaddik must do teshuvah.

Enable me to spend all my days in constant teshuvah. For "who can say, 'I have cleansed my heart, I have purified myself from sin'"[1]? My heart contains such a mixture of spiritual refuse and self-serving motives that even as I confess and say, "I have sinned before You," at that very moment, foreign thoughts and self-serving motives enter my heart, until I find that I cannot speak one word that is truly sincere. Even the ability to confess my sins in truth before You has been taken away from me.

Therefore in Your great mercy, help me to return to You always, to continually repent and fix what was lacking in my previous teshuvah, until in Your great compassion I truly attain the highest level of return. Then my heart and mind will open so that I can know Your Name.

Then I will truly know that I have not yet begun to do teshuvah in proportion to the perception of Your awesome greatness and loftiness, which You will grant me at that time! Empower me to do teshuvah after teshuvah – to continually repent for the error of having conceived Your exaltedness in a limited and corporeal manner as compared to the exaltedness that I will grasp the very next moment, again and again!

In this manner, may all my days be spent in constant teshuvah, until the day that You gather me up to You. And may I be privileged to attain the World to Come, the "day that is entirely Shabbat," entirely teshuvah.

May I destroy my evil inclination and thereby fulfill the verse: "One who offers a confession honors Me,"[2] which the sages interpret to mean slaughtering the evil inclination.[3] By doing so, I will be able to honor You in both worlds, this world and the World to Come. Help me to succeed in diminishing my own honor and magnifying Your honor.

Pour from Your great glory upon me and enable me to become a vessel for holy honor, which is for Your sake alone. May I never derive the least satisfaction from honor, and never make use of honor except for Your Name and Your service. Help me so that I never ask or expect any creature to honor me.

Help me to always be mighty, strong and tenacious in serving You, and do not let me fall. "Do not banish me from Your presence, and do not take Your holy spirit away from me."[4] Show me how to ascend and descend, so that I will be expert in the various ways of serving You – expert in advancing and expert in retreating, expert in rising and expert in falling. Then I will be able to find You everywhere, in all of life's ups and downs. As it is written: "If I ascend to heaven, You are there; and if I make my bed in the abyss, behold, You are here!"[5] May I cleave to You always, and may You fulfill in me the verse: "I am my Beloved's, and my Beloved is mine!"[6]

(LT I, 6)

■ ENTERING THE LIGHT

Notes

1. Proverbs 20:9.
2. Psalms 50:23.
3. *Sanhedrin* 43b.
4. *Selichot, Shma Koleinu.*
5. Psalms 139:8.
6. Song of Songs 6:3. The initial letters of each word in the Hebrew verse, *Ani Ledodi Vedodi Li*, spell *Elul*, the twelfth month of the Hebrew year, in which it is proper to make amends for past misdeeds and prepare spiritually for the fast-approaching new year and the Days of Awe. This "hint" is mentioned by various authorities, e.g. *Chayei Adam, Hilkhot Rosh HaShanah*, 178:1; *Kitzur Shulchan Arukh, Dinei Chodesh Elul*, 128:1, et al., evidently based on the *Siddur ARI*.

When One Plus One Equals One

The Hebrew letter alef, symbol of oneness and unification, inspires Reb Noson's prayer to attain the highest levels of teshuvah.

O God, in Your abundant mercy, please open my eyes, my heart and my ears so that I may have the sight, understanding and hearing to perceive Your greatness and exaltedness, and return to You in truth. Graciously bestow upon me knowledge, understanding and intelligence so I will understand and grasp the ways of teshuvah, and help me to walk in these ways always. For, "Your Right Hand is extended to receive penitents,"[1] and You consider teshuvah with favor, and "if not now, when?"[2]

Help me to attain perfect teshuvah, so that through me, the lower point of the letter *alef*, which represents the disciple, will be united with the upper point of the letter *alef*, which represents the tzaddik. Then the letter *alef*, which alludes to Your Oneness, will be whole.[3]

Perfect and complete through me the paradigm of the "Supernal Man who sits on the throne," as described in the prophetic vision of Ezekiel[4]; and may my *nefesh*, *ru'ach* and *neshamah* be incorporated there, in their spiritual source, now and forever.

Fill the deficiency of the moon at last, and may the light of the moon be like the light of the sun, as it is written: "And the light of the moon will be like the light of the sun, and the light of the sun will increase sevenfold like the light of the seven days of Creation."[5]

ENTERING THE LIGHT

For Your "Kingship extends over all"[6] that exists in heaven and on earth. You "perform miracles and wonders beyond searching out,"[7] and You "devise strategies so that none remains estranged"[8] from You. You "kill and give life, cast down to the abyss and elevate."[9] You bind and combine opposites together – the opposite extremes of the deepest abyss with the loftiest heights, the lower point with the upper point. Considering this, who would dare say to You, "What are You doing?"[10]

Therefore may Your compassion also reach me. Excavate a channel for me beneath Your Throne of Glory, O Benefactor of the Poor, Who listens to the cry of the destitute! Help me to truly wake up and return to You in perfect teshuvah. Let me cleave to the true tzaddikim now and forever! For, "You do not desire the death of [the sinner, who is comparable to] the dead, but that he should return from his evil path and live!"[11]

"You press a man down until he is crushed, and say: 'Return, children of man!'"[12] "Turn away from Your wrath, O God! How long must we suffer? Relent toward Your servants!"[13] "Bring us back to You, O God, and we will return; renew our days as of old!"[14]

(LT I, 6)

Notes

1. See *Likutey Moharan* I, 6:4. When a person repents, God "stretches out His Hand," so to speak, to receive his teshuvah. This is one of the key themes of the *kavanot* for the month of Elul.
2. *Avot* 1:14.
3. See *Likutey Moharan* I, 6:5. Rebbe Nachman relates the lower point of the letter *alef* to maintaining silence in the face of insult and to the Hebrew vowel *chirik*, which is represented as a dot

beneath the consonant. The upper point of the *alef* alludes to hidden mystical knowledge, to God's glory, and to the Hebrew letter *yod*. These two points are united by the diagonal line in the middle of the *alef,* which are variously related to the combination of fire and water that makes up the heavens, to the color of one's face when blushing with embarrassment, and to the letter *vav*. The unification of the lower point and the upper point of the *alef* forms the paradigm of the "man (*adam*) seated on the throne" in Ezekiel's vision (Ezekiel 1:26), which is the mystical experience. (*Adam* has the same *gematria* as *mah* [nothingness], meaning the nullification of the ego. This factor of *mah* is the precondition for the mystical experience.) Rebbe Nachman goes on to expound upon the paradigm of the *alef* as the unification of the sun and moon, Moses and Joshua, and every master and disciple.

4   Ezekiel 1:26.
5   Isaiah 30:26.
6   Psalms 103:19.
7   Job 9:10.
8   II Samuel 14:14.
9   I Samuel 2:6.
10 Paraphrase of Job 9:12.
11 Liturgy, *Yamim Nora'im*; cf. Ezekiel 33:11.
12 Psalms 90:3.
13 Psalms 90:13, according to *Targum*.
14 Lamentations 5:21.

Tishrei and Nisan

29

Two Seasons of Teshuvah

The months of Tishrei and Nisan bring great rejoicing to the Jewish people, as the holidays they contain define us as a nation and as individuals under God.

Help me to sanctify myself to an even greater degree during the two holy months that are "heads" of the year, Tishrei and Nisan,[1] for these are days of teshuvah.[2] May I return to You wholeheartedly every year at these times, and sanctify myself with an additional measure of holiness in great joy. From these two months, may I infuse myself with great holiness and sincere teshuvah, and constantly transmit them to the rest of the year.

Enable me to awaken and reveal the Ten Types of Melody.[3] May I hasten to arrange before You every day many songs and praises to Your great Name with a voice of gladness and mirth – with song, praise, melody and psalm, with strength and happiness, with all Ten Types of Song.

Thus we will finally awaken the Song of the Future World, which is a simple, twofold, threefold and fourfold song, as it is written: "The song will be yours, like the night of the festival's consecration."[4] Fulfill in us the verse: "Singers as well as flute players, all wellsprings are in you [O Jerusalem]!"[5]

Grant us the privilege of understanding the secrets of the holy Kabbalah, until we merit to grasp and to know the "Torah of the Hidden Ancient One" – the secrets of Divine wisdom destined to be revealed in time to come.[6]

(LT I, 49)

TISHREI AND NISAN

Notes

1. *Rosh HaShanah* 2a. This *Mishnah* states that several days are called "Rosh HaShanah." Among them are the first day of Tishrei, which commemorates the creation of the world, and the first day of Nisan, the day on which Jewish kings were inaugurated and from which each year of their reigns was reckoned.
2. See *Likutey Moharan* I, 49:6, citing *Tikkuney Zohar, Tikkun* 21, 45a: "The 'two arms of the King' are Tishrei and Nisan." Rebbe Nachman says this teaches that the days of Nisan are days of teshuvah, like those of Tishrei. For our sages predict, "During Nisan, we are destined to be redeemed" (*Rosh HaShanah* 11b), and the Final Redemption will only come about as a result of teshuvah (*Yoma* 65b).
3. The Ten Types of Song are the "infrastructure" of the Book of Psalms, as discussed in *Pesachim* 117a and *Zohar* III, 101a. According to Rebbe Nachman, the Ten Types of Song are: *Berakhah, Ashrei, Maskil, Shir, Nitzu'ach, Nigun, Tefilah, Hodu, Mizmor* and *Hallelu-Yah* (*Likutey Moharan* II, 92).
4. Isaiah 30:29, alluding to Messianic events (Rashi).
5. Psalms 87:7.
6. *Pesachim* 119a, citing Isaiah 23:18; *Zohar* I, 4a; ibid., III, 128a, et passim; Rabbi Moshe Cordovero, *Pardes Rimonim, Sha'ar Erkhey HaKinuyim,* 23:16; *Ohr Yakar al HaZohar, Vayikra, Naso,* et passim; *Likutey Moharan* I, 13 and 60, both discussing the concealment of the "secrets of Torah" in stories; *Likutey Halakhot, Eruvey Techumin* 5:13; ibid., *Pesach* 7:21; ibid., *Reshit HaGez* 4:1; ibid., *Edut* 4:4; ibid., *Dayanim* 3:21, et passim. The "Torah of the Hidden Ancient One" (*Atika Stima'ah*) denotes revelations from the transcendent level of Keter that are too sublime to be grasped in the present state of the world. The level of Atik is also characterized by pure kindness and mercy, with no admixture of harsh judgment whatsoever.

Rosh HaShanah
The New Year

30

The Sound of the Shofar

The sounds of the shofar resemble the sounds of a person weeping (shevarim) and groaning (teru'ah) as he contemplates his great distance from God. These expressions of teshuvah are preceded and succeeded by the clarion call (tekiah) of God accepting His people's repentance and calling them home to Him.

In Your great mercy, help us to pray with intense concentration constantly, and in particular during the "Month of the Mighty Ones"[1] – on Rosh HaShanah, Yom Kippur and Hoshana Rabbah. Help us to pray at these times with great force and intense concentration.

Prepare for us worthy prayer leaders and experts in blowing the shofar on Rosh HaShanah and Yom Kippur, who will have the ability to persuade You, appease You and arouse Your compassion.

Grant that we hear the sound of the shofar on Rosh HaShanah with unwavering mental focus, as is proper; and may we fulfill the mitzvah of hearing the shofar with all its halakhic details, fine points and intentions, as well as the complete structure of 613 mitzvot that depend on it,[2] with a good heart and great joy. May we hear the sound of the shofar directly, and not any echo of that sound.[3] Cause the holiness of the shofar blasts to enter our hearts through all the various soundings of the shofar.

Let the holy shofar blast prevail and wax strong on Rosh HaShanah! "Behold, He shouts with His voice, a voice of might!"[4] Through it, may we be awestruck before

Your presence, as it is written: "If the shofar sounds in a city, shall the people not fear?"[5] May the sound of the shofar swell mightily until it subdues, breaks and annihilates all forms of brazenness that derive from the Other Side, both the brazenness of the body and that of the "brazenfaced of the generation."[6]

May we hear all the shofar sounds correctly: the *tekiah* (long sound), *shevarim* (three broken sounds) and *teru'ah* (nine staccato sounds).[7] May we listen well and take to heart the holiness of all these sounds, until the stubbornness of our bodies is broken and our hearts are aroused in perfect teshuvah before You.

Let us be joyous and goodhearted on Rosh HaShanah throughout the day, until we weep out of joy for the sake of Your great Name. Fulfill in us the verse: "In Your Name they rejoice all through the day, and in Your righteousness they are exalted. For You are the splendor of their power, and by Your favor our glory will be raised above."[8]

Master of the Universe! You know that all our holiness depends on Rosh HaShanah, which is the beginning of the year, the first day of the year. "This day is the beginning of Your work, a remembrance of the first day,"[9] from which holiness extends to the rest of the year. Have pity on us and enable us to greet Rosh HaShanah with great sanctity and joy. Help us to purify and sanctify our thoughts on Rosh HaShanah with the highest degree of purity and holiness, for You know how important it is for us to guard our thoughts on this day.

In the merit and power of the true tzaddikim, may we complete all the holy tikkunim and unifications that we must accomplish on Rosh HaShanah and Yom Kippur, and may we transmit holiness from Rosh HaShanah to the entire year, "from the beginning of the year until the end of the year."[10]

You know that in this bitter exile, in the period known as the "footsteps of the Mashiach,"[11] we have no strength or way to fortify ourselves except through the holiness of Rosh HaShanah, this most precious gift that You have given us in Your mercy. Yet in our affliction, we lack the intellect and presence of mind to elicit the holiness of Rosh HaShanah appropriately. You know our hearts! Arise for us at this time of trouble, at the End of Days! Help us, save us and have pity on us, our Master, our Father, our King, our Rock and our Redeemer! Have mercy in the merit of the true tzaddikim of this generation, and in the merit of the true tzaddikim, "the holy ones who are in the earth"[12] – those tzaddikim whose graves we and the entire Jewish people visit and gather around in order to prostrate ourselves[13] every Erev Rosh HaShanah, where we spread forth our hands in prayer before You and beseech and entreat You with "kneeling, bowing, prostration, and with a broken and crushed heart."

Arouse the compassion of the souls of the true tzaddikim that dwell in the loftiest heights, occupying the loftiest levels of the supernal worlds. Let all the souls of the true tzaddikim descend to this world on Rosh HaShanah, where they will be together with us, in the midst of Your people, Israel, helping us to pray and entreat You on this day to subdue and banish the Evil Accuser and to shatter and nullify all aspects of brazenness of the Other Side from ourselves and from the entire House of Israel through the prayers and shofar blasts of Rosh

HaShanah. Then we will succeed in drawing holiness and purity from Rosh HaShanah upon ourselves and upon the entire Jewish people, to last the entire year.

May we rectify the "two seals" of holiness, the "seal within a seal,"[14] during the "Month of the Mighty Ones" – on Rosh HaShanah, Yom Kippur, Sukkot, Hoshana Rabbah and Shemini Atzeret. Let our voices ascend before You in favor, and may we attain perfect holy joy, constantly. "Inscribe and seal us and Your entire people, the House of Israel, for a good, long life and peace,"[15] – a God-fearing life, a true life, a life in which we will attain eternal life!

(LT I, 22)

Notes

1 I Kings 8:2 refers to the "Month of Eitanim," which we know to be the month of Tishrei. The Rabbis interpret this name as an allusion to the *eitanim* (mighty ones) – namely, the Patriarchs who were born in the month of Tishrei; see *Rosh HaShanah* 11a.

2 The Talmudic sages state that the 613 mitzvot parallel the human form. The 365 veins and tendons correspond to the 365 negative mitzvot, and the 248 limbs correspond to the 248 positive mitzvot; see *Midrash Tanchuma, Ki Teitzei*, 2; *Targum Yonatan* on Genesis 1:27; *Zohar* I, 170b; ibid., II, 25a, 228b; *Tikkuney Zohar, Tikkun* 30 (74b). Since the mitzvot, like the body, make up a unitary whole, it is axiomatic that the whole depends on each of its parts; thus the entire 613 mitzvot depend on each individual mitzvah. The Kabbalistic understanding of this paradigm is discussed by Rabbi Moshe Cordovero, *Pardes Rimonim*, 31:8; Rabbi Chaim Vital, *Sha'arei Kedushah, Sha'ar* I; Rabbi Yaakov Yosef of Polonoye, *Ben Porat Yosef*, 74b; Rabbi Shneur Zalman of Liadi, *Tanya*, chaps. 23, 24; et al.

3 One cannot fulfill the mitzvah of hearing the shofar on Rosh HaShanah through an echo; see *Shulchan Arukh, Orach Chaim* 587:1, based on *Rosh HaShanah* 29b.

ENTERING THE LIGHT

4   Psalms 68:34.
5   Amos 3:6.
6   Rebbe Nachman relates the rectification of Malkhut to the downfall of the "brazenfaced of the generation" (*azei panim*), who are false leaders, in *Likutey Moharan* I, 67:3-4; cf. *Likutey Moharan* I, 50.
7   The detailed laws of these three sounds are given in *Shulchan Arukh, Orach Chaim* 590.
8   Psalms 89:17-18, recited after the Rosh HaShanah shofar service.
9   Liturgy, Rosh HaShanah.
10 Deuteronomy 11:12.
11 See *Sotah* 49b.
12 Psalms 16:3.
13 As discussed in various Kabbalistic works, the practice of *hishtatchut* at the graves of tzaddikim usually denotes actual physical prostration. However, it also may be fulfilled by leaning on the gravestone, or even by standing or sitting near the grave. Most Breslov leaders have felt that full physical *hishtatchut* on Rebbe Nachman's grave should be performed only by an individual who has reached a high level of holiness. For further discussion of this practice, see Rabbi Shmuel Horowitz, *Tziyun HaMetzuyenet*.
14 See *Likutey Moharan* I, 22:1. The concept of a "seal within a seal" is found in the laws of *kashrut*; see *Shulchan Arukh, Yoreh De'ah* 118:1. In the Kabbalah, this term refers to the two lower sefirot of Yesod and Malkhut, in which the forces of judgment are revealed. It is also associated with Yom Kippur and Hoshana Rabbah, when Heaven's decree is "sealed" and then "double-sealed," after which it is given to the ministering angels to put into effect. Rebbe Nachman discusses how this paradigm is reflected in everyday life through the tzaddikim who rebuke the generation (corresponding to the "feet" and the "inner seal") and through faith (corresponding to the "hands" and the "outer seal").
15 Liturgy, Ten Days of Repentance *Shemoneh Esrei*.

31

The Shofar of Redemption

The shofar blasts rouse our hearts to desire and yearn for the Ultimate Redemption, when God alone will rule as King, the glory of Jerusalem will be revealed, and the Jewish people will regain the stature they once had.

In Your great mercy, allow us to hear the sound of the shofar on Rosh HaShanah from a worthy *ba'al tokei'a* (shofar blower). Empower us at the time of the blowing of the shofar to awaken the lights of the Supernal Face, which are the lights of Keter, the transcendent plane on which Your Thirteen Attributes of Mercy prevail – until the face of the *ba'al tokei'a* shines with the Light of Your Face.[1] Through these blasts, may we awaken from our spiritual sleep to renew our minds and souls at that time, and draw forth and receive new perceptions and wisdom – a new soul – from the Light of the Face, in fulfillment of the verse: "Fortunate is the nation that knows the sound of the shofar; O God, in the Light of Your Face they walk."[2]

"O Master, raise the Light of Your Face upon us and lead us up speedily to the prepared and exalted Temple!"[3] Hasten to redeem us with a complete redemption, a deliverance of body, soul and wealth, all of which are deeply in exile now. Have compassion on the refugees of Your people, the House of Israel, and quickly redeem them with an everlasting redemption, collectively and individually, physically and spiritually. Bring us our righteous Mashiach! Let the Son of David come and deliver us! Rebuild the ruins of Jerusalem, City of Justice,

ENTERING THE LIGHT

Faithful City! Illuminate us with the Light of Your Face, and speedily build our holy and beautiful Temple. There we will offer unto You our obligatory sacrifices, and be privileged to bring the Burnt Offering in its season and place, according to its rule, as well as the Incense Offering in its time.

As we do so, may we obliterate the seed of Amalek and utterly destroy the "thorns from the vineyard," thereby cutting off, uprooting and annihilating all the thistles and thorns that surround the Supernal Rose,[4] and elevating all the holy sparks from the kelipot and from the idolatrous nations. All holy sparks and souls will cleave and cling to the belief in God, and be refined and elevated higher and higher until they return, ascend and become renewed in the Light of the Face. You will prepare the Throne of David, and "the Name will be whole, and the Throne will be whole."[5] You will give us one king and one shepherd, according to Your heartfelt desire: Mashiach the son of David, King of Israel!

Thus will You reveal Your Kingship to all humanity, and magnify, elevate and exalt Your faith and Your dominion higher and higher over all creatures in the world. All of them will long and yearn for Your holy faith. "And You shall rule, O Lord, speedily, You alone, over all Your works. For Kingship is Yours, and forever and ever You will rule in glory, as it is written in Your Torah: 'God shall reign forever and ever!'[6] And it states,[7] 'And the Lord shall reign over all the earth. On that day God will be One, and His Name will be One!'"[8]

(LT I, 35)

Notes

1. The ARI states that when a righteous person sounds the shofar on Rosh HaShanah and his face reddens with exertion, he receives an influx of the Light of the Face through Binah; see *Sha'ar HaKavanot, Rosh HaShanah*, 7. Rebbe Nachman mentions this concept in *Likutey Moharan* I, 35:10, the lesson on which this prayer is based. The *Biur HaLikutim* adds that the shofar blast alludes to the call of the tzaddikim, which awakens the world to return to God and reaches all those who are lost in extraneous wisdoms.
2. Psalms 89:16, recited after the Rosh HaShanah shofar service.
3. *Yotzrot, Shabbat Shekalim Musaf.*
4. The Supernal Rose is a symbol of Malkhut, both in the metaphysical sense as the collectivity of souls, and as a euphemism for the Jewish people.
5. Rashi on Exodus 17:16, citing *Midrash Tanchuma*.
6. Exodus 15:18.
7. Zechariah 14:9.
8. Liturgy, *Aleinu*.

32

The Rosh HaShanah of the Tzaddik

The practice of traveling to the tzaddik for Rosh HaShanah brings about the unification of three roshim (heads): that of the tzaddik, who is called the rosh bnei Yisrael (head of the Jewish people); that of the individual, who comes with his own rosh, or state of mind; and that of the year, namely, Rosh HaShanah
(Likutey Moharan II, 94).

Help me, in Your great mercy, to travel to true tzaddikim for Rosh HaShanah. There all souls will merge into one encompassing unity, in great love. May we attain love of our brothers and friends and share abundant peace and love in truth, until we become spiritually fused together in love, brotherhood and friendship within the collective souls[1] of the true tzaddikim constantly, and especially on the holy days of Rosh HaShanah.

Let us merge together into the Foundation Stone, into the Holy of Holies, into the Universal Mind which is the Supernal Wisdom.[2] Through this, all harsh judgments and all constrictions of the Divine Light will be tempered, for us and for Your entire people, the House of Israel. Wherever there may be a constriction, harsh judgment or negative decree upon Your people, Israel, collectively or individually, everything will be "sweetened" and nullified by the light of the Universal Mind, the transcendental consciousness that issues forth from the House of God. Thus all harsh judgments will be sweetened at their source.

Inscribe us for a good and long life on the holy days of Rosh HaShanah, and for a good and sweet year, so that we may fulfill Your will in truth and accept the yoke of Your Kingship always. Have pity on us and help us to be what You want us to be in truth! Let our souls merge together in great love within the collective souls of the true tzaddikim, until through this we experience the greatest ecstasy, as it is written: "The light of the tzaddikim brings joy!"[3]

May we experience even more joy on the days of Rosh HaShanah, as the verse states: "Eat rich foods and drink sweet beverages, and send portions to those who have nothing prepared, for today is holy unto our Lord. Do not be sad, for God's gladness is your strength."[4]

And it is written: "Fortunate is the nation that knows the sound of the shofar; God, in the Light of Your Face they walk. In Your Name they shall rejoice all day long, and through Your righteousness they shall be exalted. For You are the splendor of their power, and by Your favor our glory will be raised above."[5]

Remove all conflict and strife from us and from Your people, the House of Israel, now and forever! Help us, for on You we rely! "Teach me Your ways; lead me in Your truth and instruct me, because You are the God of my deliverance; for You, I wait expectantly all through the day!"[6]

(LT I, 61)

Notes

1   Rebbe Nachman describes the "collective mind" or "universal mind" in *Likutey Moharan* I, 61:6, 7; ibid., II, 72. This is implicit in a number of other lessons, e.g., *Likutey Moharan* I, 65:1; II, 67;

and elsewhere, in the discussions of the *Ba'al HaSadeh* (Master of the Field), *Tzaddik Emet* (the True Tzaddik), *Yesod HaPashut* (the Simple Foundation of Being), etc. This concept appears in Ramban's commentary on the Rif, *Milchamot HaShem, Berakhot* 58a. He states that there are great sages who, due to their spiritual elevation, comprehend all viewpoints of the entire Jewish people. Their prototype is Joshua, whom the Torah describes as "the man who has *ru'ach* (spirit) within him" (Numbers 27:28), because he knew how to relate to the spirit of every individual (Rashi, ad loc.). Kabbalistic sources for the concept of the "collective mind" include *Zohar* I, 206a; ibid, III, 262b; *Tikkuney Zohar, Tikkun* 56, 92b; Rabbi Eliyahu de Vidas, *Reshit Chokhmah, Sha'ar HaYirah* 8:4 and *Sha'ar HaKedushah* 16:10; Rabbi Chaim Vital, *Etz Chaim, Sha'ar* 52, as well as his *Sha'ar HaPesukim, Bereshit* 2:3 and *Sha'ar HaGilgulim* 1. In Chassidic works, see *Sefer Baal Shem Tov, Pekudei* 1 (end), citing Rabbi Yaakov Yosef of Polonoye, *Ben Porat Yosef*; Rabbi Moshe Chaim Ephraim of Sudylkov, *Degel Machaneh Ephraim, Masei*; Rabbi Menachem Nachum of Chernobyl, *Me'or Einayim, Yitro* and *Pinchas*; Rabbi Tzadok of Lublin, *Tzidkat HaTzaddik*, 159; et al.

2 Supernal Wisdom (*Chokhmah Ila'ah*) is the Divine source of the Torah and, implicitly, all forms of wisdom (cf. *Zohar* II, 62a). According to Rebbe Nachman, the Foundation Stone in the Holy of Holies, which the *Zohar* identifies as the beginning point of the creation of the world, corresponds to Supernal Wisdom (*Likutey Moharan* I, 61:6). The tzaddik of the generation personifies the Foundation Stone and is privy to the Universal Mind. When people come to this awesome tzaddik for Rosh HaShanah, their individual minds and souls merge into the Foundation Stone, mitigating all harsh judgments.

3 Proverbs 13:9.

4 Nehemiah 8:10.

5 Psalms 89:16-18, recited after the Rosh HaShanah shofar service.

6 Psalms 25:4-5.

33

Purifying the Mind

When we free our minds of unwanted thoughts and fantasies, we create a sublime vessel for pure and holy contemplation.

May it be Your will, O Lord our God and God of our fathers, to grant us in Your abundant mercy the privilege of traveling to the true tzaddikim on Rosh HaShanah, and cleaving to them constantly. Thus may we sanctify our minds and thoughts with great holiness. Show us Your great compassion, and help us and save us from all foreign thoughts and from every kind of distorted or disturbed thinking. Graciously confer upon us wisdom, knowledge, understanding and perception, and speedily enable us to attain sanctity of the mind to the fullest.

In Your abundant mercy, sweeten and nullify all harsh decrees upon us and upon Your entire people, the House of Israel, now and forever. Let us receive the holiness of Rosh HaShanah through the true tzaddikim, and accomplish all the spiritual rectifications that we must perform on Rosh HaShanah – which is the source of Heaven's judgments for the entire year.

May our thoughts be holy and pure always, particularly on Rosh HaShanah. Bestow upon us even greater levels of sanctity of the mind at this time, and protect us and deliver us so that no foreign or unholy thought should ever enter our minds. Rather, "in Your Name we shall delight all through the day,"[1] in awe and reverence, and with the greatest holiness and purity; with holy, immaculate and luminous thoughts of the highest order.

By virtue of our spiritual bond with the true tzaddikim, enable us to accomplish all the spiritual tasks of Rosh HaShanah: to extricate all the holy sparks from the depths of the kelipot and to sweeten and nullify all harsh judgments in the world. Draw upon us "only good and kindness,"[2] deliverance and abundant mercy, "from the beginning of the year until the end of the year."[3] May we be inscribed and sealed at this time for a good and long life, and for peace; for true life, a life of fear of Heaven, a life in which we will merit to observe Your mitzvot and perform Your will in truth, wholeheartedly.

Help us to fix all the damage we caused throughout our lives until this very day. Grant us ample livelihood, mercy, life and peace, and everything good.

(LT I, 76)

Notes
1   Liturgy, Rosh HaShanah *Musaf*; cf. Psalms 89:17.
2   Psalms 23:6.
3   Deuteronomy 11:12.

34

Overcoming Obstacles

Rebbe Nachman teaches that when a person decides to travel to the tzaddik, all sorts of obstacles rise up to block him, looming ever larger the closer he comes (Likutey Moharan I, 72). *Just as we pray for the ability to visit the tzaddik, we pray that our journey will be smooth and barrier-free.*

Master of the Universe! You know the greatness of our obligation to travel to the true tzaddikim for Rosh HaShanah – and You also know how many formidable obstacles rise up to prevent us from this worthy goal.

O God, Who pities the poor, have pity and mercy on us and help us to break though all barriers. Show us Your ways, guide us in Your truth, and teach us, so that we will merit to travel to the true tzaddikim for Rosh HaShanah. Then we will truly attain sanctification of the mind. For You know that at present, during this period of travail known as the "footsteps of the Mashiach,"[1] our main support and salvation comes only from these holy days of Rosh HaShanah. Through them we seek to come close to You and to draw Your Godliness and Your Kingship upon us, both on Rosh HaShanah and during the entire year.

We do not know what is taking place in the supernal worlds on Rosh HaShanah, nor how to appease You at this time, so that we may be deemed worthy of crowning You as our King in awe and reverence. We do not know how to stand up to all our enemies and Heavenly prosecutors, "to close the mouths of our denouncers and accusers,"[2] except in the merit and power of the true tzaddikim. Upon them we rely and upon them we lean, for they wage war on our behalf, subjugating and casting down all our enemies and persecutors; and they draw upon us the holiness of Rosh HaShanah.

Therefore have mercy on us for the sake of Your Name, and take our side, so that we may overcome all obstacles and succeed in traveling to the true tzaddikim for Rosh HaShanah. Help us to bind ourselves to them in truth, to fully attain sanctification of the mind through them, to sweeten and nullify all harsh judgments, and to elicit lovingkindness.

Enlighten us so that we may recognize and perceive Your exaltedness and Your Sovereignty over us. Rule over us in Your glory speedily! "And every created thing shall know that You created it, and every formed thing shall understand that You formed it; and everything that possesses the breath of life in its nostrils shall declare: 'The Lord, God of Israel, is King, and His dominion extends over all!'"[3] Purify us and sanctify us in Your sublime holiness, now and forever. Amen, selah!

(LT I, 76)

Notes
1   See *Sotah* 49b.
2   Liturgy, *Avinu Malkeinu*.
3   Liturgy, Rosh HaShanah *Musaf*.

35

Song of the Future

Each day is truly a "new day," for God recreates the world anew every second. From this idea, we can conceive the renewal of the world during the Final Redemption, when evil will be defeated and God will reign supreme.

Grant us the merit to greet Rosh HaShanah in holiness and purity and with a whole heart. Let us draw upon ourselves the holiness of the "prayer in the aspect of judgment" of the true "Mighty Warrior," that awesome tzaddik who descends into the very throat of the Other Side in order to redeem all fallen prayers and souls[1] – and may we be worthy of all the sanctifications and spiritual healings brought about by this prayer.

Then we will fully attain *Tikkun HaBrit* (Rectification of the Covenant) and *Tikkun HaDa'at* (Rectification of the Mind). We will rectify all three "mentalities" – all three levels of the mind which are like three partitions set up against sexual immorality. When we attain higher consciousness and true intellect, lust will never dominate or affect us at all. We will all become holy and pure, and separate ourselves from this craving completely.[2]

May we attain the perfection of prayer, and may our prayers always be "expressions of compassion and supplication before the Omnipresent One."[3] Confer compassion upon us so that we will acquire true compassion, both toward worthy poor people and toward all those who need our compassion, according to Your beneficent will.

Help us to bring others back to You, to increase the number of *ba'alei teshuvah* (penitents) and converts in the world, as You desire. In this way, we will magnify Your glory and spread the knowledge of Your Godliness throughout the world, until we become worthy of true prophecy in holiness and purity. Enable us to refine the faculty of imagination so that it will be lucid, clear and radiant, making it possible for us to speak Your praises and to bless the Name of Your glory, which is exalted above all blessing and praise.

Let faith in the newness of the world, which You recreate from nothingness every instant, wax stronger and stronger, until we experience the renewal of the world in time to come when You will govern all Creation through Your Providence and wonders alone, and not at all according to the laws of nature.

Then a new song will be awakened in the world, a song of wonders, and "mountains will break out in glad song."[4] You will overcome the "heel of the Other Side," which is the heel of the wicked Esau, in fulfillment of the verse: "And his hand was grasping the heel of Esau"[5]; and You will draw upon us the waters of "the river that flows forth from Eden to water the garden."[6] Through all this, we will exude a "good fragrance," which is the manifestation of the soul that remains untainted by sin, before Your presence.[7]

(LT II, 8)

Notes

1 In the last lesson of his life (*Likutey Moharan* II, 8, *Tiku/Tokhachah*), Rebbe Nachman describes the awesome spiritual task of a Mighty Warrior who seeks to vanquish the Other Side and

redeem all fallen prayers and souls that the latter has "swallowed" throughout the course of history. He does so by praying a "prayer in the aspect of judgment" – a prayer that does not appear to be an appeal for mercy, as prayer should be (*Avot* 2:13). The Other Side attempts to swallow this prayer of the Mighty Warrior as well. But this prayer turns out to be a prayer of *deveykut* in disguise, so the Other Side cannot swallow it. Rather, it sticks in the throat of the Other Side, which chokes and begins to regurgitate all the prayers and souls it has ever swallowed, until it finally spits up its very life force. This brings about the Final Redemption and awakens the Song of the Future World (*Tikkuney Zohar, Tikkun* 21, 51b). The Mighty Warrior is a thinly-veiled reference to Rebbe Nachman himself, and the "prayer in the aspect of judgment" alludes to his mission on behalf of the Jewish people and the world while dying, and even posthumously. Rebbe Nachman hinted to the latter meaning with his declaration, "I have finished, and I will finish [in the future]!" (*Chayey Moharan* 322).

2   There are numerous levels of *Tikkun HaBrit*; see *Likutey Moharan* I, 11:5; ibid, II, 5 and 32; *Sichot HaRan* 86. The most basic level is that of marriage and conformity to the laws of *Taharat HaMispachah* (family purity) and marital conduct, as detailed in halakhic works. However, we are also enjoined to "sanctify ourselves in the realm of the permissible." To the extent that we succeed in curbing our physical desires, we become liberated from the shackles of the body and may enter the realm of the holy. The highest degree of *Tikkun HaBrit* was reached by Moses, who overcame the desire for sexual relations completely, transmuting these energies to the spiritual plane; see *Mishneh Torah, Yesodei HaTorah* 7:6.

3   *Avot* 2:13.
4   Paraphrase of Isaiah 44:23.
5   Genesis 25:26.
6   Paraphrase of Genesis 2:10.
7   We have rendered this line interpretively, based on *Likutey Moharan* II, 8.

36

Healing the Eyes

To merit seeing the holy visage of the true tzaddikim at Rosh HaShanah, as well as to behold the beauty of holy objects like the tefilin, we must repent for all the wrongdoing we have done in God's sight.

In Your great mercy and kindness, grant me the privilege of traveling to the true tzaddikim on Rosh HaShanah each and every year. May I be counted among the simple good Jews who gather with the true tzaddikim on Rosh HaShanah.

You alone know the great loftiness of the convocation of Your people, Israel, when they flock to the true tzaddikim on Rosh HaShanah. You alone know how much You take pride in us and derive great and awesome delight every Rosh HaShanah from the holy gathering of the Jewish people with the true tzaddikim. In Your mercy, allow that we too may be part of this supernal pride and delight! May no one deter us, may nothing hold us back, and may no hardship in the world stop us!

Rather, grant us the merit of traveling every year to join the devout Jews who make up the holy and awesome gathering beside the true tzaddikim on Rosh HaShanah. May You always take pride in us, and confer upon us constantly the holiness of the Land of Israel.[1]

Allow us to gaze upon the splendor and beauty of the faces of the true tzaddikim who personify *kelilat yofi* (consummate beauty).[2] For the tzaddikim contain within themselves all the pride and delight of the entire Jewish people, which You receive through them, since they are constantly occupied with bringing others close to You. Grant me the privilege of gazing upon their faces at all times, especially on the holy days of Rosh HaShanah that are designated for Your glorification. At that time, their faces shine intensely with the collective light of the supernal pride and gratification produced by the holy gathering of all those who come to them.

Please, God, in Your great compassion, permit us to gaze upon the beauty of their holy and awesome faces in truth, so that we too may receive and draw upon ourselves a wondrous illumination of this supernal pride,[3] until we are able to draw upon ourselves constantly the sanctity of the holy tefilin. Then the beauty of the holiness of the tefilin will shine forth from our eyes, and wherever we set our gaze, that place will become sanctified with the holiness of the Land of Israel. Anyone who has ever tasted the holiness of the Land of Israel will sense its holiness wherever they meet us, and they will recognize, know and discern that we spent Rosh HaShanah with the true tzaddikim.

Master of the Universe! God full of mercy! Have pity on the cries of the Shekhinah, which cries with a bitter voice over our evil deeds! "My head aches, my arm aches!"[4] Who can bear the sound of Her cries? You alone know their great bitterness. Have mercy, have mercy, and deliver us right away from evil deeds and evil thoughts. Enable us to truly return to You in the merit and power of the true tzaddikim. Cause the Shekhinah to take pride in us from now on, and to derive great delight and gratification from us always – from each and every one of us!

Help us to attain perfect teshuvah and speedily fix all the damage we have caused in Your sight, from our youth until today. For we have sinned greatly by gazing beyond the bounds of holiness, which led us to innumerable sins and transgressions, and much spiritual damage. We have done that which is evil in Your sight. Woe unto us, for we have sinned! We damaged our holy eyes, which have their origin in the "eyes of God," in Divine perception.[5] They might have been privy to see God's delight in us, to behold the faces of the tzaddikim, and to transmit the holiness of the Land of Israel wherever they gazed. But because of our wrongdoing, we took these holy and awesome eyes and gazed with them at all sorts of sights, until we wound up wherever we wound up, due to our many transgressions.

Merciful One, teach us the way to fix all this! Help us and save us so that we may seek and find true tzaddikim with whom we share the same "soul root,"[6] and let us travel to them again and again, particularly on Rosh HaShanah, the designated time of the holy gathering. Let us be numbered among the good Jews who congregate with the tzaddikim, and in so doing return to You sincerely, in wholehearted teshuvah.

Allow us to gaze upon their holy faces and thereby fix all the spiritual damage that we have brought about in Your sight, from our youth until today. Shine upon us the light of the holy pride You take in us, which emanates from their holy faces. May we then transmit the holiness of the Land of Israel wherever we gaze, until all places where the Jewish people dwell become sanctified with the holiness of the Land of Israel. Amen!

(LT II, 29)

ROSH HASHANAH

Notes

1 The Land of Israel is the focal point of *Hashgachah Pratit* (Divine Providence), which is an aspect of the *Tikkun HaMalkhut* (Perfection of God's Kingship). *Tikkun HaMalkhut* is also the central theme of Rosh HaShanah; thus, these two paradigms are essentially bound up with one another. In *Likutey Moharan* II, 8, delivered on the last Rosh HaShanah of his life, Rebbe Nachman discusses the full manifestation of Divine Providence in time to come as occurring hand in hand with the extension of the holiness of the Land of Israel throughout the world (ibid., section 10).

2 See Ezekiel 27:3, 28:12; Lamentations 2:15: Psalms 50:2. Reb Noson also seems to be playing on the similarity between *kelilat* (consummate or perfect) and *kelalut* (universality). The true tzaddik is said to possess a *neshamah kelalit* (collective soul), which includes all souls; see for example *Likutey Moharan* I, 61; ibid., II, 72; et passim.

3 Reb Noson links the Hebrew word for pride, *hitPa'aRut*, to the beauty (*Pe'eR*) of the tefilin in the following sentence.

4 *Sanhedrin* 46a.

5 One reason the Torah declares that man was created "in the Divine image" (Genesis 1:26) is because human traits and abilities parallel Divine attributes. For example, the *Zohar* states: "Chesed is the right arm, Gevurah is the left arm ..." (*Tikkuney Zohar, Patach Eliyahu,* Introduction). This parallelism enables us to be instruments of God's will and, ultimately, to acquire knowledge of God to the extent that is humanly possible.

6 Since Cain and Abel were the first two children of Adam and Eve, all souls derive from them and inherit certain tendencies from them. In this context, either Cain or Abel is identified as a person's *shoresh neshamah* (soul root). Rabbi Chaim Vital lists some of the characteristics by which one can determine if his soul derives primarily from Cain or Abel (*Sha'ar HaGilgulim, Hakdamah* 36). For example, those rooted in Cain tend to be more mechanically inclined and oriented toward physical action, while those rooted in Abel tend to be more verbal. These two categories of Cain and Abel are each subdivided into seventy roots, which

are subdivided further, until the full array of "soul roots" numbers 600,000. From there, the souls continue to subdivide beyond measure. This collectivity of souls is compared to a tree with roots, branches, twigs, buds, leaves, etc. The souls of certain tzaddikim are called "roots" or "branches" in the sense that other souls of more limited capacity are derived from them. Yet despite this vast diversity and complexity, all souls ultimately make up one harmonious whole.

Aseret Yemei Teshuvah

The Ten Days of Repentance

37

"Seek God When He May Be Found"

In His great mercy, God allows us to repent and be cleared of all wrongdoing during the very first days of the year, so we can begin the new year in the best possible way.

Have mercy on us and enable us to return to You in sincere and complete teshuvah, all the more during the Ten Days of Repentance. May we fix all the damage of the entire year during these days, especially damage of the covenant (sexual immorality).

Please have compassion in Your abounding mercy, and enable us to sanctify ourselves with the greatest, most awesome, additional measure of holiness during these Ten Days of Repentance, when You are available to all who seek You in truth, as it is written: "Seek God when He may be found, call upon Him when He is near!"[1] In Your abundant mercy and compassion, You gave us the precious gift of these Ten Days of Repentance, knowing that we are but flesh and blood, "formed of clay,"[2] and, "There is no man so righteous on earth that always does good, and does not sin."[3]

Therefore "You prepared a healing and balm before the sickness,"[4] and in Your great mercy and profuse kindness, You made known and gave to us at the very beginning of the year these ten holy days from Rosh HaShanah to Yom Kippur. At this time, we are given additional strength to return to You in perfect teshuvah, and to repair all the spiritual damage and all the sins, transgressions and wrongful deeds of the entire year.

ASERET YEMEI TESHUVAH

Please grant us merit, please show us grace, and do not let us lose this precious gift! For due to our many sins, the Evil One also arises against us during these Ten Days of Repentance, so that many years have come and gone and we still have not attained perfect teshuvah. Even more, due to our many sins, we have added much more damage during these very days of repentance, as well as on Rosh HaShanah, Yom Kippur, Sukkot, Shemini Atzeret and Simchat Torah. We have failed to observe all these holy days properly, without any deficiency; and we have done grievous harm on them, too – in thought, speech and action, unintentionally and intentionally, by coercion and by complicity.

"What further justification do I have to cry out any more to the King?"[5] "My transgression is too great to bear,"[6] the depth of my sin too great to describe. If not for Your compassion and mercy, "I would perish in my affliction."[7]

Merciful One, starting now, enable me to search out and find everything I have lost, from my first day on earth until today! Starting now, help me to attain purity and holiness throughout the year, and even more on these Days of Awe. May I attain complete teshuvah during the Ten Days of Repentance, fix everything I have destroyed, and completely repair all damage of the covenant, in truth.

In this way, I will steadily perfect the "seal of holiness" until the arrival of the great and awesome fast of Yom Kippur, the "Shabbat of Shabbats," the Day of Forgiveness of sin and transgression, the Day of Atonement from all iniquity. Then, at last, the "seal of holiness" will be perfected to the ultimate degree!

(LT II, 5)

Notes

1. Isaiah 55:6.
2. Paraphrase of Job 30:19.
3. Ecclesiastes 7:20.
4. *Megillah* 13a.
5. II Samuel 19:29.
6. Genesis 4:13.
7. Psalms 119:92.

Yom Kippur
Day of Atonement

38

The Gift of Forgiveness

Every year God holds out to us the chance to wipe the slate clean and remove the shame and guilt that weigh us down from our misdeeds.

Grant me the merit to receive the holy day of Yom Kippur with great sanctity, joy and gladness. May I perfectly fulfill all five afflictions[1] on Yom Kippur, as is proper, and pray the five prayer services of Yom Kippur with the most awesome and intense concentration. May I perform all the detailed confessions (*viduy*) and regret my past sins with complete sincerity, repudiating in truth my evil ways and my evil and confused thoughts. May I accept upon myself with firm resolve not to return to my former folly, and no longer do what is evil in Your sight, as I have done in the past. May I return to You in wholehearted teshuvah, in joy, fear and love, and cry profusely from joy!

God full of mercy! Allow me to experience the awesome and exalted holiness of Yom Kippur, the one day of the year that You chose for Your people to forgive their sins and atone for their iniquities! Have mercy on us and allow us to properly receive this awesome day, to return in true repentance, so that You will forgive and atone for all our sins, transgressions and iniquities that are so profound and numerous and weighty... countless as the sands of the seashore!

In the merit of the intrinsic holiness of this sacred day, and in the merit of the holy fast of this awesome day, the "day of the fast of atonement," may we subjugate within

YOM KIPPUR

ourselves all desires and direct them only to You. Let us completely nullify every sort of will before Your will, until we possess absolutely no desire or will contrary to Your will. Then whatever we do will openly reflect Your intention, and we shall never depart from Your will, "neither to the right or the left."[2] Then, in Your mercy, You will "nullify the will of others before our will"[3] and put a stop to every sort of strife in the world, whether conflict between people or conflict within ourselves – for right now "there is no peace in my bones because of my sin."[4]

Whenever I wish to undertake some holy enterprise, I must face the greatest obstacles, seemingly without number! And the most formidable obstacles are those of the mind and heart. However, it is possible to nullify them all through the holy fast of Yom Kippur, the day that incorporates all the days of the year, as it is written: "Your eyes saw my unshaped form, and in Your book all were recorded; though they were fashioned over many days, to Him they are one."[5] On this, our sages expound: "This is Yom Kippur."[6]

Have mercy on us and enable us to truly attain complete teshuvah throughout the year, and in particular on Yom Kippur. Help us to complete the fast of Yom Kippur in the most awesome state of holiness, and with the greatest happiness and joy, so that we will be able to sanctify ourselves from now on, and know how to conduct ourselves in the matter of fasting throughout the year. May our actions truly accord with Your beneficent will, so that we will be "neither ashamed nor disgraced, nor shall we stumble ever again!"[7]

(LT I, 103)

Notes

1. The five afflictions are: to fast from dusk (*shkiah*) until the appearance of three stars (*tzeit hakokhavim*) the following night; to refrain from bathing, anointing the body, and wearing leather shoes; and to abstain from marital relations. These five afflictions apply equally to men, women, boys over the age of thirteen and girls over the age of twelve. One who feels physically unable to fast should consult a rabbinic authority. A person whose health would be jeopardized by fasting may actually be forbidden to do so.
2. Paraphrase of Deuteronomy 17:11. In Kabbalistic terminology, the "right" represents the attribute of Chesed (Kindness), while the "left" represents the attribute of Gevurah (Judgment).
3. Paraphrase of *Avot* 2:4.
4. Psalms 38:4.
5. Psalms 139:16.
6. Rashi on Psalms 139:16.
7. Paraphrase of *Birkat HaMazon* (Grace After Meals).

39

Reviving the "Dead Days"

Fasting is not meant to be an external show of piety, but a tool to arouse inner feelings of remorse and resolve to change our ways. This emotional prayer verbalizes our deepest desire to use Yom Kippur and other fast days as vehicles for real change.

Merciful One! You know how many days lie dead wherever they are stored away like so many corpses, due to the countless evil deeds that I committed in the course of my life until today. You know how I robbed the very life from these days with wanton cruelty. Not only did I deprive these days of vitality by my neglect of Torah and Divine service, but I also drained them of their inherent vitality altogether through the sins that I performed on those days.

The tikkun for all these dead days requires many fasts, as You have revealed to us through Your holy sages. Have mercy on me, and help me and save me with Your wondrous kindness, so that I might remedy all these dead days through the power of the holy fast of Yom Kippur, as well as through all the holy fast days that I may be privileged to complete in my lifetime.

May I fast so much that I need to draw sustenance from the days of my infancy, from the very nourishment of my mother's milk. In this way, may I succeed in resurrecting and repairing all the days that have passed, from my first moment until now. When my time comes to leave this world, may I appear before You with all the days of my life in great holiness; and may all my days be complete, holy, pure and perfected, according to Your beneficent will, "so that I not arrive embarrassed before You."[1]

Help me, help me! Save me, save me! Perform lifesaving wonders for me so that I should not be like the dead, God forbid! "I shall not die, but I shall live, and relate the deeds of God!"[2] Gladden my soul, which is so wretched and oppressed, through the many fasts You will mercifully enable me to complete from now on; and may I greatly strengthen myself in this.

God of mercy, help me! God of deliverance, deliver me! Have compassion on me, All-Compassionate One! O God, "Who acts with goodness toward the guilty, Who has treated me entirely with goodness,"[3] Who granted me the privilege of being a Jew, "separated me from those who wander in error,"[4] and did not make me a member of another nation. Confer even more good upon me, and give me the strength to separate myself entirely from the false pleasures of this world. Help me to be patient and forbearing with all my might, to overcome my natural inclinations and rule over my spirit, and to strengthen myself at all times – until I can shut my eyes to the illusions of this world entirely and fast many fasts, even from one Shabbat to the next!

In Your mercy, please receive these fasts with love and favor, and bring me closer to You with great compassion. Gladden my soul constantly, so that in the power of the true tzaddikim I will succeed in repairing all the damage I caused throughout my life. May I merit to perceive You in truth, and constantly serve You in truth – myself, my children, and all of my descendants, forever!

(LT I, 103)

Notes
1 *Zohar* III, 287b.
2 Psalms 118:17.
3 Paraphrase of *Birkat HaGomel* (Blessing of Thanksgiving)
4 Liturgy, *Uva LeTzion*.

40

Yom Kippur Paves the Way for Chanukah

When we achieve the heights of joy and purity that can be ours on Yom Kippur, we enable our souls to receive the light of holiness and redemption on Chanukah.

In Your great mercy, allow us to experience the holiness of Chanukah. Every year, through our supplications and requests for good on the holy day of Yom Kippur, may we persuade You to forgive the sins and transgressions of Your people, the House of Israel, and remove our guilt each year.

"Please forgive the transgression of this nation, according to the greatness of Your kindness, just as You have forgiven this people, from Egypt until now! And God said: 'I have forgiven according to your word!'"[1]

Please forgive, please overlook, please atone for all the sins, misdeeds and iniquities that we have committed before You, from our childhood until today.

O God, in Your kindness and great mercy, erase my wrongdoing! "Wash me thoroughly from my iniquity, and from my sin, cleanse me!"[2] Grant us the forgiveness of Yom Kippur, and may we receive the holiness of the days of Chanukah, which commemorate the rededication of the Holy Temple. And during Chanukah, may we draw upon ourselves the sanctity of the Holy Temple!

(LT II, 7)

Notes

1 Numbers 14:19-20.
2 Psalms 51:4.

41

Magnifying God's Name

Yom Kippur is the gateway to a world saturated with God's light and beneficence.

"Act for the sake of Your Name, and sanctify Your Name."[1] Be with us and help us to return to You speedily, sincerely and wholeheartedly, particularly during the holy and revered Days of Awe – which are the days of Elul, Rosh HaShanah, the Ten Days of Repentance and Yom Kippur. These days make up the "forty days of Divine favor" during which You became reconciled to Moses our teacher and gave him the Second Tablets. Then, on the last day, You became reconciled to him completely, and told him with joy: "I have forgiven according to your word!"[2] This day was the holy, awesome, sublime day of Yom Kippur, a day that You designated for forgiveness and pardon for all generations. All this You did for the sake of Your great and holy Name, by which we are called!

Have mercy on us and help us to receive these holy and awesome days with the greatest sanctity and purity. During these days, may we repent completely and sincerely, and rededicate ourselves wholeheartedly to walk in Your ways, to fulfill Your mitzvot, to labor in the study of Your Torah all the days of our lives, and to pray with concentration and "pour out our hearts like water before God."[3] May "streams of water flow from our eyes"[4] because of our sins, transgressions and iniquities, and because of the multitude of our afflictions – until we appease and placate You, and You will forgive, pardon and atone for all the wrongdoings we have committed in Your sight. Uproot, destroy and nullify all harsh decrees against us, both those which the Heavenly court has already decreed, and those which are under consideration for the future. And may we merit that through us, Your great Name will be magnified and sanctified constantly.

Just as You became reconciled to Moses our teacher, telling him joyously on Yom Kippur, "I have forgiven!" so may You be reconciled toward Your people, Israel, on Yom Kippur. Answer us by declaring, "I have forgiven!" with great joy and gladness.

Thus, Your Name will be magnified forever, until it is truly befitting to call the day after Yom Kippur, *Gott's Nomen* (God's Name).[5] For we have been taught that God's Name is magnified forever on this day, because of the forgiveness and pardon of Yom Kippur, and because all harsh decrees and suffering are nullified. May Your Name achieve greatness to the fullest degree, as You have made known to us through Your holy sages, may their merits shield us. "I will rejoice and exult in You, I will sing praise to Your Name, O Most High!"[6]

(LT II, 54)

Notes

1 Liturgy, Daily Prayers.
2 Numbers 14:20.
3 Lamentations 2:19.
4 Lamentations 2:18; cf. Psalms 119:36.
5 According to the Baal Shem Tov, the day after Yom Kippur is known as "God's Name" because on that day, in the third blessing of the *Shemoneh Esrei*, we stop referring to Him as *HaMelekh*

HaKadosh (the Holy King) and instead conclude the blessing with the words, *HaEl HaKadosh* (Holy God); *Sefer Baal Shem Tov, Yom Kippur* 51, citing Rabbi Avraham Warman of Butchatch, *Eshel Avraham, Orach Chaim* 624; also cf. *Likutey Maharich*, Vol. III, p. 679, which mentions this tradition. Rebbe Nachman offers a mystical explanation in *Likutey Moharan* II, 66 to the effect that when God becomes reconciled with Israel, His Name is made great; see there.

6   Psalms 9:3.

Sukkot
The Festival of Booths

42

In the Sukkah's Protective Shadow

Our temporary abode for the week of Sukkot reminds us that true security comes from faith in God, not from money or possessions.

In Your great mercy and abundant kindness, allow me to fulfill the mitzvah of dwelling in the sukkah properly, according to its detailed laws and intentions, as well as the complete structure of 613 mitzvot that depend on it,[1] with joy and a good heart, and with perfect *kavanah*.

Through the mitzvah of dwelling in the sukkah, may we draw upon ourselves the holiness of the Seven Clouds of Glory that hovered over the Israelite camp in the desert,[2] and "may You spread over us Your Sukkah of Peace."[3]

Confer upon us the perception of these holy transcendent lights when we perform the mitzvah of dwelling in the sukkah in holiness, purity and joy.

Shield and protect us, and save us from every enemy and predator – both our physical adversaries and spiritual adversaries. Remove the Accuser from before and after us, and conceal us in the shadow of Your wings![4]

(LT I, 21)

Notes

1. See p. 89, note 2.
2. *Sukkah* 11b.
3. Liturgy, Evening Prayers.
4. Ibid.

43

Becoming One with God

Rebbe Nachman teaches that by praying with force (Hebrew: ko'ach, which has the gematria of twenty-eight), a person draws energy from the twenty-eight letters of Creation that make up the first verse of Genesis, propelling him to the highest levels of holiness.

O God Who dwells eternally on high, help us! Holy One, above all holiness, sanctify us! Lord, God of truth, confer Your holiness upon us in truth! Raise up Your Sukkah which has fallen again and again, beyond all count and measure, to the point that no one can erect it but You alone, in Your abundant compassion and Your hidden store of kindness. Speedily cause it to stand again, one stage after the next, from a deep abyss to a tall colossus.

Merciful One, Beneficent One! Turn my heart from evil to good; direct my thoughts and feelings to You in truth, according to Your benevolent will. Enable me to sanctify myself with all aspects of holiness, particularly in the "covenant of the tongue" and the "covenant of the flesh."[1]

Help me, so that no false word ever escapes my lips, nor any improper utterance. May I always guard the gates of my mouth! Grant me the privilege of praying before You with all my strength, with the greatest sincerity and concentration. Thus may I merge within You at the hour of prayer, to the extent that my words of prayer are the very words of the Shekhinah speaking through me![2]

May I awaken the twenty-eight letters of the first verse of Genesis, which are the root of the Ten Sayings by which the universe was created.[3] Then You will pour forth Your abundant kindness upon us, spread over us Your Sukkah of Peace, embrace us with Your Right Hand and let us take refuge in Your holy shadow. Protect us and save us from our enemies, adversaries and persecutors, both physical and spiritual, and in the shadow of Your hand conceal us. Fulfill in us the verse: "His Hand is beneath my head, and His Right Hand embraces me."[4]

Subdue, cast down, overpower, uproot and nullify the "sukkah of heresy," the "sukkah of idolatry," of which it states: "For their mouths speak falsehood, and their right hand is a right hand of deceit."[5] Remove falsehood from the world and cause truth to prevail. Raise up the fallen sukkah of David and fulfill in us the verse: "True speech is established forever, but a false tongue is only for a moment."[6]

Conceal us in Your holy Sukkah and cover us with Your holy shadow. Save us from quarrelsome tongues, so that they have no power over us at all. Uproot falsehood and reveal the truth to the world – and grant me the privilege to go to the Land of Israel, the Holy Land, speedily, without another moment's delay!

(LT I, 48)

Notes

1 *Sefer Yetzirah* 6:4; also see Rabbi Eliyahu de Vidas, *Reshit Chokhmah, Sha'ar HaKedushah* 11:7, 12, to the effect that sinning through speech and through sexual immorality reinforce one another. Rebbe Nachman discusses this in *Likutey Moharan* I, 19; et al.

2 In *Likutey Moharan* I, 22:10, Rebbe Nachman states that when a tzaddik reaches a state of nullification within the Infinite Light, his Torah perception becomes the actual "Torah of God" and his prayer becomes the actual "Prayer of God." Rebbe Nachman also discusses the paradigm of becoming a channel for holy speech during prayer in *Likutey Moharan* I, 48, the lesson on which this prayer is based.
3 See *Zohar* II, 245a.
4 Song of Songs 2:6.
5 Psalms 144:8.
6 Proverbs 12:19.

44

"Sukkah-Consciousness"

Elevating us to higher levels of God-consciousness, the mitzvah of sukkah gives us the merit to build our own homes on a foundation of holiness and purity.

"One thing I ask of God, only this shall I seek: that I may dwell in the House of God all the days of my life; thus to gaze upon God's pleasantness and to meditate in His Sanctuary. For He will hide me in His Sukkah on a day of evil; He will conceal me in the shelter of His tent; upon a rock He will elevate me!"[1]

Master of the Universe! Have mercy on me in Your profound compassion and abundant kindness, and allow me to fulfill the mitzvah of dwelling in the sukkah at its proper time, with all its details, fine points and intentions, as well as the complete structure of 613 mitzvot that depend on it,[2] with a good heart and great joy. May I imbue myself with the holy consciousness and the wondrous spirit of kindness and giving that You confer upon Your people, Israel, during the holy days of Sukkot, through the awesome mitzvah of dwelling in the sukkah. For then "the mother bird hovers over her chicks," and You spread over us Your Sukkah of mercy, life and peace.

Compassionate One! Have mercy on us for the sake of Your Name! You know my heart – how extremely far I am from the mitzvah of sukkah, and how many supplications and requests and words of persuasion beyond measure I must pray and plead before You, that I might attain this higher consciousness and spirit of kindness. Thus I may acquire true human perception, so that I may speedily leave the status of an animal to become a human being, and take pity on myself from now on and no longer behave like an animal. Instead, may I speedily attain true perception, which is the defining characteristic of man.

Let me derive nourishment from the spiritual channels for human sustenance, and no longer from those channels designated for the sustenance of animals. May I speedily go out and rise from the category of an animal to that of a human being!

Master of the Universe! Master of the Universe, "Who is good and shows goodness to all, and Whose mercy is upon all His works!"[3] Have pity and compassion toward the animals and wild creatures, and prevent me and the entire Jewish people from any deficiency in performing the mitzvah of dwelling in the sukkah. Then we will constantly derive nourishment from the *shefa* (Divine energy) designated for humans, which derives from the paradigm of the sukkah; and we will not need to derive nourishment from the *shefa* designated for animals, God forbid, nor take what belongs to them and thus bring about the premature death of animals and wild creatures, God forbid. As it is written: "Man and beast You deliver, O God!"[4] And: "Blessed be the fruit of your womb, and the fruit of your land, and the fruit of your animals; the offspring of your cattle and the flocks of your sheep and goats."[5]

Therefore may it be Your will to confer upon us true Divine perception in full measure through the mitzvah of dwelling in the holy sukkah, so that no danger will befall us – physically, spiritually or monetarily – in the construction of our own homes, God forbid. On the contrary, may everyone build his home in great holiness and purity, with "wisdom, understanding and knowledge,"[6] in fulfillment of the verse: "Through wisdom, a house is built, and through understanding, it is established; and through knowledge, its chambers become filled with precious and pleasant treasures."[7]

Let us build our homes in the name of God, in order to engage in Torah and prayer within and to show hospitality to worthy guests. May each of our homes be called "a house of Torah and prayer" and "a gathering place for the wise," where the Name of the Eternal One will be invoked.

(LT I, 145)

Notes

1 Psalms 27:4-5.
2 See p. 89, note 2.
3 Paraphrase of Psalms 145:9.
4 Psalms 36:7.
5 Deuteronomy 28:4.
6 Paraphrase of Exodus 31:3 and 35:31. Reb Noson alludes to the qualifications of Betzalel ben Uri, who oversaw the construction of the vessels for the Tabernacle in the desert, the precursor of the Holy Temple.
7 Proverbs 24:3-4.

45

Good Dreams

The rewards for observing the mitzvot of Sukkot exceed our imagination ... even to the realm of our dreams.

Grant us the privilege of receiving the festival of Sukkot in great holiness and purity, with profound joy and gladness, for the sake of Your great and holy Name. Let us rejoice and delight in Your deliverance with all our might! May we be *akh samei'ach* (utterly happy)[1] during the days of Sukkot, the "season of our rejoicing,"[2] and celebrate, sing and dance for joy with every fiber of our beings!

Allow us to fulfill the mitzvot of dwelling in the sukkah and waving the Four Species perfectly and wholeheartedly, with great happiness, according to all their detailed laws and holy intentions, as well as the complete structure of 613 mitzvot that depend on it.[3] In the merit of the mitzvah of sukkah, may we prepare and strengthen the holy angel that presides over our dreams – and thus receive our dreams through an angel, and not through any unholy channel. May our food be spiritually refined and pure, with no admixture of dross or waste at all, so that our food does not harm us in any way. And may all our dreams enter our minds for the good!

(LT II, 5)

Notes
1 Liturgy, Yom Tov *Shemoneh Esrei*.
2 Liturgy.
3 See p. 89, note 2.

46

A Spiritual Harvest

We long for the day when we will display God's pride in us and our pride in Him, and God will spread His Sukkah of Peace over us and over the entire world.

Help us to fulfill the mitzvah of dwelling in the sukkah at its proper time, according to all its detailed laws and holy intentions, as well as the complete structure of 613 mitzvot that depend on it,[1] wholeheartedly and with great joy. Cause us to cleave to You through Your holy mitzvot, and embrace us with Your holy Right Hand, with love and great compassion.

Spread over us Your Sukkah of Peace, and conceal us in the shadow of Your wings! Through the holy and awesome mitzvah of the sukkah, cause us to dwell in Your shadow – in the shadow of holiness and the shadow of faith.

Reveal and make known before the eyes of all that Your profound love and compassion rest on us; and may everyone acknowledge and proclaim: "For God chose Jacob for His own, Israel as His treasure."[2] Indeed, "God's portion is His people; Jacob is the rope of His inheritance."[3]

We will take pride in You constantly, and You will take pride in us, as it is written: "You have set apart the Lord this day to be your God; to walk in His ways, and observe His decrees, His commandments and His ordinances, and to hearken unto His voice. And God has set you apart this day to be for Him a treasured nation, as He declared to you, and to observe all His commandments;

and to make you supreme over all the nations that He has made, for praise, for renown and for splendor, so that you will be a holy people unto the Lord, your God, as He has spoken."[4]

Let us always serve You sincerely and wholeheartedly, and reveal Your Godliness and Your Sovereignty to all humanity.

Favorably incline the hearts of earthly kings, government officials and advisors toward us, and abolish all harsh decrees against us. Fulfill the verse: "For He will hide me in His Sukkah on a day of evil; He will conceal me in the shelter of His tent; upon a rock He will elevate me!"[5]

Master of all the world, Who is full of new expressions of mercy every moment, "I spread forth my hands unto You; my soul is like an arid land unto You."[6] Help us and save us in the merit of the tears of the true tzaddikim and of all Israel! May the true tzaddikim finish the work they undertook to perfect all our souls, speedily and completely, according to their holy goodwill toward us, and not according to our evil deeds!

Help us for Your sake and for their sake, and cause us to return to You speedily in perfect teshuvah. Lead us in Your truth and instruct us, "for You are the God of my deliverance. For You, I have hoped all the day."[7]

Instill in us true simplicity and wholeheartedness. "Do it for the sake of Your Name! Do it for the sake of Your Torah! Help us, O God of our deliverance, for the honor of Your Name! Save us, and atone for our sins for the sake of Your Name!"[8] "Blessed is the Lord of Israel, Who alone performs wonders! Blessed is His glorious Name forever;

and may the entire world be filled with His glory. Amen and amen!"[9]

(LT II, 57)

Notes

1. See p. 89, note 2.
2. Psalms 135:4.
3. Deuteronomy 32:9.
4. Deuteronomy 26:17-19.
5. Psalms 27:5.
6. Psalms 143:6.
7. Psalms 25:5.
8. Liturgy.
9. Psalms 72:18-19.

47

Prayer for the Four Species

The unique mitzvah of waving the Four Species in all six directions (north, south, east, west, up and down) draws and transmits Divine perceptions to all levels of Creation.

Grant us a beautiful etrog on the holy festival of Sukkot. May we acquire a truly beautiful, kosher etrog, possessing every sort of beauty, as well as a kosher and beautiful lulav (palm branch), aravot (willows) and hadasim (myrtles).

May we perform the mitzvah of waving the Four Species in its proper time, to the ultimate perfection, in the greatest holiness and purity, with love and awe, and with the greatest joy and gladness.

May we recite the full Hallel with true intentions, with all Four Species, as well as the Hoshana prayers – performing all the *na'anu'im* (wavings) and the awesome *hakafot* (circular processions) with love and awe and the greatest joy, with true concentration of the heart, with wondrous *deveykut* and intense fervor, for the sake of Your great, holy and awesome Name, in truth and wholeheartedness, according to Your desire and the desire of the true tzaddikim!

By performing the *na'anu'im,* may we transmit an illumination of higher consciousness to all six directions, corresponding to the six sefirot of Chesed, Gevurah, Tiferet, Netzach, Hod and Yesod; and from thence, may we transmit this higher consciousness to the aspect of Malkhut (Kingship).

ENTERING THE LIGHT

In this way, Your Kingship will be revealed to the eyes of all, and we will make known to all humanity Your might, glory and the splendor of Your dominion. "And every created thing shall know that You created it, and every formed thing shall understand that You formed it; and everything that possesses the breath of life in its nostrils shall declare: 'The Lord, God of Israel, is King, and His dominion extends over all!'"[1]

(LT II, 57)

Notes
1   Liturgy, Rosh HaShanah *Musaf.*

48

True Beauty

Man is the paragon of Creation ... and the tzaddik is the paragon of man. As we gaze at the beauty of the etrog, we pray that the beauty of the true tzaddikim will attract and guide the rest of humanity toward a meaningful relationship with God.

Grant us the privilege of fulfilling the mitzvah of the etrog in its proper time. May we always acquire a beautiful etrog, kosher and beautiful in every way, to the ultimate degree of perfection and beauty.

Reveal the splendor and beauty of the holiness of Your people, Israel, to the world – especially the beauty of the holiness of the true tzaddikim and devout Jews who strive to fulfill the Torah's ideals. Then all humanity will long and yearn to become part of them, to become subsumed within their name and their beauty; and all humanity will follow in their holy ways to perform Your will in truth, all of their days, forever!

(LT II, 33)

Hoshana Rabbah
Shemini Atzeret
Simchat Torah

49

When Heaven's Decree is Sealed

On Rosh HaShanah the Heavenly judgment is writted, on Yom Kippur it is signed, and on Hoshana Rabbah and Simchat Torah it is sealed. Kabbalistically, the beating of the willows on Hoshana Rabbah and dancing with the Torah on Simchat Torah "sweeten" the judgment.

Sanctify us on Hoshana Rabbah and Simchat Torah,[1] which correspond to the paradigms of speech without da'at and speech imbued with da'at. Grant us the privilege to study Your holy Torah constantly. Even when we fail to understand the words of Your Torah clearly and correctly, may we nevertheless exert ourselves to read them and keep studying, even without understanding. In Your mercy, accept this effort as well and rejoice in our words of Torah, even when they lack comprehension. Plant from them mighty trees surrounding that stream of Binah, which are called "willows of the brook."[2]

Awaken Your great mercy toward us, stand by us, and open the eyes of our minds so that we may go forth from darkness to light! Enlighten our eyes with the light of Your Torah so that we may know, understand and comprehend all the words of Your Torah lucidly and according to their true meaning – all the detailed laws of the Torah, and all the ways of the Torah. May we strive therein along a paved path until we succeed in planting a Supernal Tree of Life that will be a cure for everything![3]

Grant that every year we fulfill all the mitzvot related to these holy days of Hoshana Rabbah and Simchat

HOSHANA RABBAH ▪ SHEMINI ATZERET ▪ SIMCHAT TORAH

Torah, and rejoice on these days with the ultimate joy and gladness, in true ecstasy, and become sanctified in them with great holiness. Thus we will accomplish all these tikkunim and more on these awesome holy days, when the seal is affixed for the Heavenly decree and the tikkun that was initiated on Rosh HaShanah and Yom Kippur.

Enable us to accomplish the seven *hakafot* of Hoshana Rabbah with the holy and awesome Four Species to the ultimate degree of perfection, according to Your beneficent will. May we scream and cry out to You, and pray the Hoshana supplications with a whole heart, from the very depths of the heart, as befits us to cry out for Your deliverance on this awesome day when Heaven's holy, profound and dreadful judgment is concluded. May we perform the mitzvah of striking the five willow branches on the ground, which was the custom of Your prophets of old, with great sanctity and joy. In this way, we will sweeten all judgments to the ultimate degree and bring about the perfect unification of the Holy One, blessed be He, and His Shekhinah through our efforts on Shemini Atzeret and Simchat Torah.

(LT I, 93)

Notes

1. Hoshana Rabbah falls on the seventh day of Sukkot. On the following day, the festival of Shemini Atzeret begins. In the Land of Israel, Shemini Atzeret is a one-day festival and is combined with the celebration of Simchat Torah. Outside the Land of Israel, Shemini Atzeret is a two-day festival; on the second day, Simchat Torah is celebrated.

2   The *Zohar* states: "There are some who study the Torah and stammer due to lack of knowledge (*da'at*). Yet each word ascends on high and the Holy One, blessed be He, delights in it. He receives it and plants it on the banks of that brook [a symbol for the sefirah of Binah], so that from these words mighty trees are created, called 'willows of the brook'" (*Zohar* III, 85b). Rebbe Nachman relates the paradigm of words without da'at to Hoshana Rabbah, and that of words with da'at to Simchat Torah, in *Likutey Moharan* I, 74, the lesson on which this prayer is based.

3   The same passage from the *Zohar* goes on to state: "Worthy are those who know the paths of Torah, who engage [in fulfilling it] on a straight path. They plant a Tree of Life on high, which has the power to heal" (ibid.). The *Zohar* implies that by studying the Torah in order to fulfill it, one establishes a spiritual connection to the Tree of Life described in the first chapter of Genesis, which is the source of healing.

50

The Tikkun of Shemini Atzeret

False leaders have done more to mislead and destroy the Jewish people than any non-Jewish enemies. The holiness of Shemini Atzeret can give us the merit to be guided by true and worthy leaders.

In the merit of the holiness of Shemini Atzeret, grant us the tikkun of holy judgment and discrimination, and through this, save us always from damaging the covenant and from nocturnal emissions, God forbid. In the cycle of the year, Shemini Atzeret is compared to conception.[1] Therefore we beseech You: May the holiness of Shemini Atzeret protect us, so that our marital relations will be conducted in sanctity and lead to the conception and birth of children, without any destruction of seed, God forbid.

Protect us and save us from unworthy rabbis and *dayanim*, and remove their power and dominance from the world. Rather, in Your abundant mercy, confer upon us and the upon entire Jewish people truly qualified rabbis and dayanim who will establish the law and render absolutely correct judgments. Thus, we will attain the tikkun of judgment and the tikkun of the covenant to perfection, in all aspects, according to Your beneficent will.

Have mercy on us for the sake of Your Name, and fulfill all our requests for the good, whether we are on the level of "children" or "servants" before You. "If we are like children, have mercy on us as a father has mercy on his children; and if we are like servants, our eyes look to

ENTERING THE LIGHT

You beseechingly, until You show us grace and bring our judgment to light, O Mighty and Holy One!"[2]

(LT II, 5)

Notes

1 In the writings of the ARI, Shemini Atzeret is compared to conception and Pesach is compared to birth; see Rabbi Chaim Vital, *Pri Etz Chaim, Sha'ar HaLulav,* ch. 8. Rebbe Nachman weaves these concepts into one of his major Rosh HaShanah lessons, *Likutey Moharan* II, 5:14.

2 Liturgy, Rosh HaShanah.

51

The Unbroken Circle

Shemini Atzeret and Simchat Torah are times of great joy and celebration. May we merit to carry this happiness with us into the rest of the year!

May we rejoice on Shemini Atzeret and Simchat Torah with endless gladness and joy for the privilege of being part of the Jewish people, and for having received the Torah through Moses, Your prophet, the "trusted member of Your household."[1]

"Fortunate are we, how good is our portion; how pleasant is our lot, and how beautiful is our inheritance!"[2] Fortunate are we, in that we have been granted all this great and awesome goodness! Help us to absorb this happiness into our hearts throughout the entire year, and especially on the holy day of Simchat Torah. May we constantly exult in this great joy, as is truly befitting.

Let us perform the *hakafot* with the Torah scrolls on these holy days with gladness that reaches to infinity! May nothing unworthy be commingled with our festivity, and may no obstruction or interference be allowed to disturb or inhibit our ecstasy. Enable us to rejoice and delight in You with the most wondrous *deveykut* and intimacy, with "great love" and "eternal love"[3] – with endless joy beyond all bounds!

Grant us the privilege of completing the yearly cycle of reading the holy Torah and beginning it anew at this time, with love, awe and great gladness. May we accept upon ourselves anew the mitzvah of studying the Torah day and night without any ulterior motives, and fulfill all the Torah's words with love.

ENTERING THE LIGHT

God full of mercy, have mercy on us and fulfill our requests for the good! Then our souls will ascend in holiness to their source, which is the holy sefirah of Chokhmah, by virtue of our efforts to study the Torah in a spirit of holiness and purity until we truly comprehend it. Enable us to perceive You in truth and reveal Your Godliness to the world. May Your great glory be magnified and sanctified through us always, and may Your glory fill all the world.

(LT I, 93)

Notes

1 Numbers 12:7.
2 Liturgy, paragraph before *Shma* in *Seder HaKorbanot*.
3 According to the ARI, *ahavah rabbah* (great love) corresponds to the World of *Atzilut*, while *ahavat olam* (eternal love) corresponds to the World of *Beri'ah*; see Rabbi Chaim Vital, *Sha'ar HaKavanot, Drush Kavanot "Yotzer."*

52

Connecting Sukkot, Simchat Torah and Shavuot

Sukkot is the prelude to Simchat Torah, and Simchat Torah to Shavuot, as we endeavor to be worthy of the great gift of Torah.

Through the mitzvah of sukkah, may I be privileged to rejoice greatly on Simchat Torah, to complete the yearly cycle of reading the Torah and to begin again, with gladness and mirth. "Let us celebrate with this Torah with all our might, for it is our source of strength and light!"[1]

Stand by us constantly, year after year, so that we may fulfill the mitzvah of dwelling in the sukkah to such a degree of perfection that, as a result, we merit to receive the Torah anew, each and every year. For the Torah comes forth from the sukkah, which represents the Holy Temple. By entering the sukkah, we become worthy for Torah to come forth from our very beings. Every Jew can personify and express the Torah, since "the Torah, Israel and the Holy One, blessed be He, are one."[2]

Through the holiness of the festival of Sukkot, confer upon us the holiness of the festival of Shavuot, the holiness of the month of Sivan during which the Torah was given, and the holiness of receiving the Torah anew!

(LT I, 145)

Notes

1 Liturgy, Simchat Torah.

2. A Kabbalistic axiom based on *Zohar* I, 24a: "The Holy One, blessed be He, and the Torah are one," and *Zohar* III, 73a: "Three levels are bound to one another: the Holy One, blessed be He, the Torah, and Israel." Parenthetically, Rabbi Aharon of Zhelikhov, *Ohr HaGanuz LeTzaddikim, Miketz* (p. 28), cites a related teaching of the Baal Shem Tov: "The letters of the Torah are God's vessels and chambers. By concentrating on them, one can infuse them with an emanation of the Supernal Light, as the *Zohar* states: 'The Holy One, blessed be He, and the Torah are one.' A person must put his entire power of thought into the letters, for this is the soul itself. This is the *deveykut* implied by 'The Holy One, blessed be He, the Torah, and Israel are one.'" Cf. *Likutey Moharan* I, 281, where Rebbe Nachman asserts that even the most ordinary Jew can gain sublime insights by gazing fixedly at the letters of the Torah.

Chanukah

53

Prayer Before Lighting the Menorah

Prior to kindling the Chanukah lights, we pray that all our mitzvot will kindle the light of perfection, to illuminate the whole world.

Master of the Universe! Help us in Your great mercy to fulfill the mitzvah of lighting the Chanukah candles in its proper time, in a perfect manner, in a spirit of holiness and purity, and with intense concentration. May we be privileged to perform these tikkunim which we have mentioned before You through the mitzvah of the Chanukah candles; and may our fulfillment of this mitzvah be considered in Your sight as if we had done so according to all its details, fine points and intentions, as well as the complete structure of 613 mitzvot that depend on it.[1]

May the light of the holiness of our mitzvot shine before You throughout all the worlds! By performing this mitzvah, as well as all the mitzvot, scriptural and rabbinic, may we perfect all the worlds entirely.

Let us perform all these mitzvot in love and awe and with great joy, to the highest degree of perfection, until we succeed in eliciting peace from You and transmitting it to all the worlds, in fulfillment of the verse: "God will give strength to His people; God will bless His people with peace."[2]

"May the One Who makes peace in His heavens bring peace to us and to all Israel. Amen."[3]

(LT I, 14)

Notes

1 See p. 89, note 2.
2 Psalms 29:11.
3 Liturgy, *Kaddish*.

54

Experiencing the World to Come in This World

The mitzvot of Chanukah have far-reaching consequences, setting us squarely on the path to experience the delight of the World to Come in this world.

Enable us to fulfill the mitzvot of Chanukah with joy – to praise You and bless You, and to recite the full Hallel with fervor and delight, in holiness and purity. In Your abundant mercy, You established for us the eight days of Chanukah so that we might praise and exalt Your great Name; days on which we may experience the delight of the World to Come.

Grant us the privilege of truly fulfilling Your mitzvot, until we reach the point of constantly experiencing the delight of the World to Come by praising Your great and holy Name – especially during the days of Chanukah, which our sages designate as "days of thanksgiving."[1]

Then we will come close to You in truth. We will know and perceive You, and we will praise You and bless You in truth forever, for You are entirely good. As it is written: "Praise God, for He is good, for His kindness is everlasting!"[2]

(LT II, 2)

Notes

1. *Shabbat* 21b; cf. *Likutey Moharan* II, 2, the lesson on which this prayer is based.
2. Psalms 136:1.

55

Open Eyes

While they radiate only tiny pinpricks of light in this physical world, the Chanukah candles illuminate a spiritual gateway to exalted levels of enlightenment and Divine perception.

Master of the Universe! Enable us to fulfill the mitzvah of lighting the Chanukah candles in its proper time, in holiness and purity! Through the sanctity of this mitzvah, may we also attain "open eyes." Enlighten our eyes so that we may perceive our true lowliness and deficiency and Your greatness and exaltedness. May our faith be purified and refined until it is free of any trace of disbelief or confusion, God forbid. Then we will be able to receive all Your beneficence and abundant kindness. Fulfill in us the verse: "It is good to thank God and to sing praise to Your Name, O Exalted One; to recount Your kindness in the dawn and Your faith in the nights!"[1]

Open for us all the gateways of holiness so that we may serve You in truth. "Open the gates so that the righteous nation, keeper of the faith, may enter!"[2] "Open for me the gates of righteousness; I will enter them to praise God! This is the gate of the Lord, the righteous shall enter it."[3] Amen, may this be Your will!

(Tefilot VeTachanunim I, *Tefilah* 10)

Notes
1 Psalms 92:3.
2 Isaiah 26:2.
3 Psalms 118:19-20.

56

Igniting the Inner Flame

Rebbe Nachman teaches that God can be found in every created thing and in every circumstance and event in our lives. By "reading" the messages He sends us, we can use the physical world as a stepladder to draw close to the Divine.

Master of the Universe! Enable us to fulfill the mitzvah of lighting the Chanukah candles in its proper time! May it be in Your sight as if we had fulfilled this mitzvah with all its details and fine points, and as if we had meditated upon all the holy intentions implicit in the mitzvah of lighting the Chanukah candles. Confer upon us an illumination of the holiness of the *Mochin HaKedoshim* (the holy sefirot of Chokhmah, Binah and Da'at) from their supernal source, in an aspect of "drawing down abundant holiness and igniting the flame."[1] Help us to expand our minds and deepen our perceptions until we can understand all the holy hints that You have concealed in the thoughts, words and actions that You have prepared for us every moment, according to the person, place and time. In all of them You have written holy messages, telling us how to come closer to You.

Thus we may bind our thoughts to the World to Come in a detailed manner, through the textures of this world, until we succeed in elevating and causing to stand the "feet of holiness" – the lower levels of the animating Divine wisdom that is garbed within all mundane things.

(*Tefilot VeTachanunim* I, *Tefilah* 23)

Notes

1 *Zohar* III, 37a; *Likutey Moharan* I, 54:11.

57

The Light of God's Face

According to the ARI, 370 Lights emanate from the transcendent level of Arikh Anpin, the persona of Keter, figuring in the Kabbalistic meditations for Chanukah.

Master of the Universe! Enable me to light the Chanukah lights with oil, and may You in turn confer upon us a great illumination of the sublime transcendent lights known as the "370 Lights of the Face." Fulfill in us the Priestly Blessing: "May God cause His Face to shine unto you and be gracious to you."[1] Grant us an ample livelihood, with great holiness, in such a manner that while we are eating and striving to earn a living, we will experience a revelation of these transcendent lights, which are the Light of the Face. As it is written: "He causes vegetation to sprout for the animal, and plants through man's labor, to bring forth bread from the earth; and wine that gladdens the heart of man, to make the face glow from oil, and bread that satisfies the heart of man."[2]

(*Tefilot VeTachanunim* I, *Tefilah* 37)

Notes
1 Numbers 6:25.
2 Psalms 104:14-15.

58

Bringing Down the Light

No matter to what depths we have fallen, the tzaddikim can rescue us by "shining" down the light of Divine perception to heal our souls.

Help us, O Lord our God, to receive the holiness of the days of Chanukah in sanctity and purity, and with true joy. Grant us the privilege of lighting the Chanukah candles every night, as You have commanded us through our holy rabbis of blessed memory – to begin by lighting one candle on the first night, and to add another candle on each succeeding night, until the eight days of Chanukah are complete. For You have already made known to us through our holy sages that through the holiness of the Chanukah candles, we imbue our minds with perceptions of Godliness. The *tzimtzumim* (constrictions) of the Infinite Light which they represent produce the spiritual illumination transmitted by all holy lights and candles. This is the paradigm of "eliciting abundant holiness and igniting flames and radiant lights."[1]

Shine upon us the light of the holy anointing oil,[2] enlightening us with perceptions of Godliness in a miraculous and wondrous way. Thus may we illuminate and kindle the holy candles which contain all spiritual unifications and transmissions of Divine consciousness – so that their light will reach even people like us who occupy the nethermost rung, which corresponds to "below ten handbreadths."[3]

Through the tikkunim of the miracle of Chanukah, may we too experience this light through the power of the preeminent tzaddikim who transmit perceptions of the supernal light to us, even in our lowly condition.

They heal us from sicknesses of the soul which threaten to overwhelm us, to the point that "our souls abhor all food, and we have reached the gates of death."[4] For we know in our hearts how fiercely these sicknesses attack us, and how every day our souls grow weaker, due to the multitude of our sins. However, in Your great mercy, You ennoble us with the holiness of this awesome mitzvah of lighting the Chanukah candles. Through this mitzvah, the true tzaddikim transmit the radiance of Divine perception even to such spiritual invalids as us, and they bring down this lofty light into the darkness that pervades our bodies because of our evil deeds. These tzaddikim "shine" to us, so that we might take to heart their holy words; they enliven us with their words, and in so doing, transmit the holy light of the Chanukah candles to the depths of darkness.

May we firmly believe that without a doubt, we can go forth from darkness to light with this mitzvah, in the merit of the true tzaddikim who illuminate the earth and all who dwell upon it! Fulfill in us the verses: "Even when I walk in the valley of the shadow of death, I shall not fear evil, for You are with me."[5] "Though I sit in darkness, God is a light unto me."[6]

Instill compassion into the hearts of the true tzaddikim toward the entire Jewish people and toward me, so that they will mercifully draw all of us closer. May they lower themselves to our level, shine their lights upon us, and reveal flashes of Divine perception, even to people like us, and may they succeed in healing our souls. May they fulfill the mitzvah of visiting the sick by attending our ailing souls every day! Thus they will give us new life and revive us with spiritual delicacies, until we finally return to You in perfect teshuvah when we accept and follow all their holy advice, which is a powerful remedy for our souls.

Illuminate our souls with the wondrous radiance of Divine perception in the aspect of Chanukah! Revitalize our wisdom in holiness, and grant us life from the Light of the Face as a result of our rejoicing in the mitzvot. Gather together the mitzvot that we perform on the Three Pilgrim Festivals and in their merit, may we participate in the re-dedication of the Holy Temple, which is the channel for the illumination of the Light of the Face!

"The Light of Your Face, O Master, lift up to us."[7] "May God favor us and bless us; may He cause His Face to shine among us, selah."[8] "Shine Your Face upon Your servant; save me in Your kindness"[9] – so that through the lighting of the Chanukah candles I will be privileged to draw the Light of the Face from the Holy Temple in order to enliven the sefirah of Malkhut, and thereby receive perceptions of Godliness.

"Let Your Face shine upon Your servant, and teach me Your ordinances."[10] "And every created thing shall know that You created it, and every formed thing shall understand that You formed it; and everything that possesses the breath of life in its nostrils shall declare: 'The Lord, God of Israel is King, and His dominion extends over all!'"[11]

In Your mercy, grant us the opportunity to give tzedakah, especially during the days of Chanukah, so that through us Your Face will shine. And by virtue of the tzedakah that we give to the poor when they come to our homes, may we receive the Light of the Face of the Living King.

CHANUKAH

In the merit of this tzedakah, may we draw closer to the true tzaddikim who reveal Your light by making the necessary *tzimtzumim* and vessels to illuminate even our souls, which are so far from holiness that by rights we should be treated as outcasts. Nevertheless, with great self-sacrifice, they labor all their days out of compassion for us and for all Israel – even those who are most distant – in order to bring us closer to God. They reveal new and wondrous *tzimtzumim* by which it is possible to reach anyone who wishes to enter the realm of holiness.

Have mercy on us and allow us to come close to tzaddikim like them. In Your mercy, put an end to the dispute, which was produced by our sins, surrounding those tzaddikim who strive to reach out to us. For this is why there is such great opposition to them, even from other great tzaddikim: The Divine attribute of judgment garbs itself in these opposing tzaddikim because of their fierce holiness, which prevents them from being able to tolerate the world, due to our transgressions and unworthy deeds.

Although the truth is with them, You have already made known to us that in Your beneficence, You do not desire to reject us, God forbid. On the contrary, You always wish to judge us favorably, despite the foulness of our sins. You always wish to show compassion toward us, even to the "worst of the worst." Therefore You create ways of fixing our damage, and garb the lights of holiness in such wondrous garments and constrictions that these lights can shine to us as well.

Thus the tzaddikim continue to transmit the Divine light to lower levels, in increasing degrees of holiness, more and more every day; and they continue to elevate all fallen souls, imbuing them with perceptions of Godliness through holy *tzimtzumim*, until finally they will heal all afflicted souls in the world. Therefore have mercy on us, and abolish all strife surrounding these true tzaddikim, and allow us to draw close to them. Let them remove all the shame and disgrace that has befallen us due to our sins, bring us back in complete teshuvah, and draw us close to You in truth!

(*Tefilot HaBoker, Tefilah* 4)

Notes

1 *Zohar* III, 37a; *Likutey Moharan* I, 54:11.
2 Exodus 30:25-31 describes the anointing of the Mishkan, Holy Ark, Table, Menorah, Incense and Sacrificial Altars, and various vessels, as well as the anointing of Aharon and his sons, with this "oil of sacred anointment." Later, this oil would be used to anoint kings of the Davidic dynasty and High Priests. Based on various passages from the *Zohar*, Rabbi Moshe Cordovero explains that the oil of sacred anointment is a vehicle for the transmission of Chokhmah through the channels of Chesed and Gevurah, and from thence to Yesod and Malkhut; see *Pardes Rimonim, Erekh HaKinuyim, Sha'ar* 22:21. Rebbe Nachman mentions the oil of sacred anointment in his interpretation of the Rabbah Bar Bar Chana story in *Likutey Moharan* I, 4:9.
3 The Talmudic sages state that the Shekhinah does not descend below ten *tefachim* (handbreadths) (*Sukkah* 5a). However, due to the unique spiritual power of Chanukah, it is a mitzvah to place the candles (which represent the light of the Shekhinah) below ten *tefachim* if possible. For the details of this law, see *Shulchan Arukh, Orach Chaim* 671:6. Reb Noson expounds on various facets of this theme in *Likutey Halakhot, Hashkamat HaBoker* 4:10; ibid., *Chanukah* 2:1, 3:1, 6:1; ibid., *Hashmatot LeHilkhot Chanukah*; ibid., *Shilu'ach HaKen* 5:7; ibid., *Kaley Ilan* 1:1; ibid., *Shluchin* 3; ibid., *Matanah* 5:65; et passim.
4 Paraphrase of Psalms 107:18.

5   Psalms 23:4.
6   Micah 7:8.
7   Liturgy, *piyut* for *Shabbat Shekalim*.
8   Psalms 67:2-3.
9   Psalms 31:17.
10 Psalms 119:135.
11 Liturgy, Rosh HaShanah *Musaf*.

Seventh of Adar
Yahrtzeit of Moses

59

Searching for the Moses of Our Generation

Like trusting sheep, the Jewish people only await the shepherd's call to gather together and return home to their Master.

"Give ear, O Shepherd of Israel, Who leads Joseph like a flock; [O God] Who is enthroned upon the *Keruvim*, shine forth!"[1]

Master of the Universe, Sovereign, Leader and Ruler – All-Merciful One! You had pity on us and sent us a deliverer and master, the "redeemer of Israel and its holy one,"[2] Moses our teacher, may peace be upon him, who brought us out from darkness to light, gave us the Torah, enlightened our eyes, and made known to us the truth of Your holy faith. In his awesome and towering spiritual stature, he was able to enlighten even those who were most lacking in merit, such as us today, to make known to all Your greatness and Your might, to open the eyes of the blind and to give sight to the eyes of all Israel. He was even able to deepen the perception of those who personified the aspect of the "feet," so that they too could grasp the true purpose of all existence – to know You through all created things, and to come close to You, and to cleave to You in truth.

Fortunate is the generation that had such a leader! Fortunate are the eyes that were privileged to behold him! Fortunate are the ears that were privileged to hear the "words of the Living God"[3] from his awesome and holy mouth, for the very Shekhinah spoke through his throat![4]

Now, O Lord our God, our Father, heed our urgent plea! Open Your eyes and behold our devastation! Have mercy on us, and show us and teach us what we can do now, what we can accomplish now, and to whom we may turn for help. "Tell me, O You Whom my soul loves: Where will You graze Your flock? Where will You give them rest from the noonday sun?"[5]

Let us know which path to follow in search of a true leader such as Moses. Owing to our profound lowliness and weakness today, when the inner light of our faces no longer shines, no one can help us except that exceptional master and true leader who will be an aspect of Moses our teacher, peace be upon him – one who will also be able to illuminate us with holy perceptions so that we might reach the true goal, which is to know and perceive You through the entire panorama of Creation. For You formed all things only so that, through them, man might come to know You. This is the essential purpose of all Creation.

How can we find such a leader as this? Where? Where is he? "Where is the place of [God's] glory?"[6] Where is the advice and strategy that will enable us to find him?

Today there are also tzaddikim and leaders, may God grant them life and length of days and years. Yet don't they all admit to themselves, without exception and without shame, that they lack the power I have described before You? They lack the power of Moses to enlighten us with this higher perception, so that each one of us will recognize the true goal in this world through the panorama of all worldly existence, this being the purpose for which we were formed. Now, what can be done? Who will arise on our behalf? "Who will preserve Jacob, for he is small?"[7]

Master of the entire world, Who has mercy on the earth, Who has mercy on all creatures, Who "led Your people like a flock by the hand of Moses and Aaron"[8] – where is Your compassion for Israel, Your holy nation, now? For whom would You abandon this tiny flock? For whom would You repudiate us, powerless as we are, unworthy as we are today? "Behold, we stand before You, impoverished and empty,"[9] our faces blackened from sin, our stature bent from transgression. To whom should we flee for help? "Do You thoroughly despise Yehudah? Do You loathe Zion?"[10]

If You would renounce Your people, Israel, God forbid, have You not already promised us that even when we reach our lowest point of decline in this deep exile, in body and soul, as we have today, You will not reject us nor despise us forever? As it is written: "But despite all this, while they are in the land of their enemies, I will not be revolted by them, nor will I reject them to obliterate them, to annul My covenant with them – for I am the Lord their God."[11] And it is written: "But God did not say to erase the name of Israel from under the heavens."[12] And it is written: "For God will not forsake His people for the sake of His great Name, because God has sworn to make you as a people unto Him."[13] And it is written: "For God will neither forsake His people nor abandon His inheritance."[14]

With these and many other such promises, You assured our ancestors that You would help us and save us in every generation. Where is Your compassion now? Where are Your wondrous deeds? Why are we left "like a flock without a shepherd?"[15] Have mercy on us! Have mercy and compassion, and enable us to pray and plead before You at length, to cry out, scream bitterly, and weep profusely before You every day, until You graciously answer us, and pity us, and grant us a "Shepherd of Israel," a true leader, a compassionate leader, like Moses our teacher. Provide us with a faithful shepherd who can engage in our spiritual perfection and bring us back to You in truth, who can illuminate even us with his holy perceptions and open the eyes of our minds in great holiness and purity, so that even we may grasp the ultimate purpose of all created things in the world and truly recognize You, come close to You and cleave to You forever!

Help us to receive Shabbat in a befitting manner, with great joy and gladness and wondrous *deveykut,* according to Your beneficent will, until we come to know and grasp the ultimate purpose of the creation of heaven and earth, even in this world. Let us know and perceive You through all created things, according to Your will and the will of those who truly revere You. Then we will be privileged to experience the "day that is entirely Shabbat and contentment for the eternal life."[16]

All-Merciful One! O God, open our eyes so that we may see, understand and perceive the absolute truth. Show us how we should conduct ourselves now, in order to seek and find a true leader such as Moses, who can bring us to the ultimate true goal during this lifetime – for "we have none to rely on, except our Father in Heaven."[17]

"We are the clay, and You are our Potter, and all of us are Your handiwork."[18] "Upon You the helpless rely; for the orphan You have been the helper."[19] You alone know the hidden recesses of our hearts, and how to help us now in all matters, particularly in this matter on which everything depends: to find that true leader who is an aspect of Moses our teacher, who is capable of bringing us to the ultimate, true and eternal goal speedily during our lifetimes. Do what is good in Your sight, for we have cast our entire burden upon You!

"As for me, I shall always hope,"[20] "until God looks down from Heaven and sees."[21] Then He will return to us, and have mercy on us; and like a father to a son, He will bestow His favor upon us. He will restore the crown to its former glory and give us a shepherd, according to His heart, and speedily fulfill the verse: "I will appoint for you shepherds according to My heart, and they will tend you with knowledge and perception."[22]

Speed and hasten our Redemption, and sent us our righteous Mashiach! Quickly fulfill the verse: "I will establish over them a single shepherd, and he will tend them – My servant, David. He will tend them, and he will be a shepherd to them. And I, the Lord, will be a God to them, and My servant David, a prince among them. I, the Lord, have spoken!"[23]

And it is written: "They shall no longer be contaminated with their idols, with their abhorrent things, and with their iniquities. I will rescue them from all their dwelling places in which they had sinned, and I will purify them. They will be a nation unto Me, and I will be a God unto them. My servant David will be king over them, and there will be one shepherd for all of them. My ordinances they will follow and My decrees they will heed and perform."[24] "God of Hosts, lead us back, and cause Your Face to shine, and we shall be delivered!"[25]

(LT II, 28)

Notes

1. Psalms 80:2.
2. Isaiah 49:7.
3. Deuteronomy 5:22.
4. In the words of the *Zohar* III, 232a: "The Shekhinah speaks through the mouth of Moses"; cf. ibid., III, 306b; *Tikkuney Zohar, Tikkun* 38 (end). Essentially, the Shekhinah is bound up with all holy speech; e.g. *Tikkuney Zohar, Tikkun* 18 (33b), *Likutey Moharan* I, 38:2, ibid., I, 78.
5. Song of Songs 1:7.
6. Liturgy, *Musaf Kedushah*. In this context, God's glory rests on the tzaddikim as it rested on Moses. Thus, in searching for the tzaddik, one is in fact searching for God's glory.
7. Amos 7:2.
8. Psalms 77:21.
9. Paraphrase of *Selichot*.
10. Jeremiah 14:19.
11. Leviticus 26:44.
12. II Kings 14:27.
13. I Samuel 12:22.
14. Psalms 94:14.
15. Numbers 27:17, et al.
16. *Tamid* 7:4, cited in Shabbat morning service, *Ein K'Elokeinu*.
17. *Sotah* 9:11.
18. Isaiah 64:7.
19. Psalms 10:14.
20. Psalms 71:14.
21. Lamentations 3:50.
22. Jeremiah 3:15.
23. Ezekiel 34:23-24.
24. Ezekiel 37:23-24.
25. Psalms 80:8.

Purim

60

Asking for Miracles

Reb Noson evokes the connection between Purim and Pesach in several different contexts in this emotional prayer, pleading with God to deliver us today with the same wonders and miracles that He performed in days of old.

May it be Your will, O God and God of our fathers, Who performs miracles and wonders in every generation, fighting our battles and adjudicating our judgments, avenging our grievances, repaying all those who hate us, and compensating us for our sufferings – shower Your abundant mercy upon us and deliver us with Your awesome wondrousness, so that we may receive and uphold the holy days of Purim in their season, as is befitting. Let us fulfill all the holy mitzvot performed on Purim in great holiness and purity, joyfully and wholeheartedly, "with mirth, glad song, pleasure and delight," according to all their detailed laws, fine points and intentions, as well as the complete structure of 613 mitzvot that depend on them.[1]

Master of the Universe! You have already made known to us that the miracles and wonders You performed for our ancestors, which our holy festivals commemorate, are all reenacted and revealed and shine forth in every generation, in every person and time. We need to draw the holiness of Purim and all the festivals, as well as the miracles and wonders that took place at these times, in every year, in every generation, and in every person.

Therefore I have come before You Who performs miracles and wonders in every generation, as well as in every day and every hour, with this request: Teach me, instruct me, be gracious to me, and grant me the privilege to rejoice on Purim truly and completely; to rejoice with all my heart and soul on the holy days of Purim, each and every year, with boundless joy!

Through the joy and holiness of Purim, may I draw upon myself and upon all Israel the holiness and purity of the *Parah Adumah* (Red Heifer),[2] which purifies from contact with the dead. For You commanded us to read the Torah account of the *Parah Adumah* after Purim; and You disclosed to us that through Purim, we merit to attain the spiritual purification of the *Parah Adumah*, so that we will be in the necessary state of purity to receive the holiness of the *Korban Pesach* in its season.[3]

Master of the Universe! You know how deeply we have fallen during this bitter exile, and how many spiritual sufferings have overwhelmed each Jew, including myself. The depths of the sea threaten to drown me; they engulf me from all sides. I am in such dire straits that I cannot think of any way to solve my problems and be saved from all this. I need miracles and wonders and awesome salvations, such as those You performed for Israel long ago – awesome miracles and wonders that have not been seen since the days of Mordekhai and Esther, when the evil Haman, may his name be blotted out, rose up against us. As You informed us through Your holy sages of blessed memory, the miracle of Purim was greater than all the miracles You ever performed. And, "All the festivals will be canceled in time to come, but the days of Purim will never be canceled."[4] And, "At first all beginnings were from Pesach, since all the holidays commemorate the Exodus from Egypt; but now... ."[5]

Master of the Universe, Ruler of the entire world, Master of Wonders, Who causes all deliverances to sprout forth! You know the truth, that of all the miracles and wonders You have performed for us – the Exodus from Egypt, the battle with Amalek in the days of Moses and in the days of Mordekhai and Esther, and all the miracles and wonders You have performed on our behalf during the days of Chanukah, as well as in every generation – the greatest miracle and salvation is the deliverance of the soul. For the jealousy and hatred of all our adversaries and persecutors, both physical and spiritual, focus squarely on our belief in the Lord our God, and our desire to walk in Your holy ways, to fulfill Your awesome mitzvot, and to reveal and publicize the truth of our faith in Your Divinity, Your Providence and Your Sovereignty. For this reason exclusively, "not one alone arose against us to destroy us; rather, in every generation, they have arisen against us to destroy us, but the Holy One, blessed be He, rescued us from their hands."[6] Display Your zealousness to save us from all our troubles, and perform miracles and wonders to preserve Your Torah and mitzvot. Do not allow Your Torah to cease from the world, God forbid, as is the desire of the anti-Semites and atheists who are instruments of the kelipah of Haman-Amalek.[7]

Now, what can I say before You, Who dwells on high, and what can I relate before You, Who sits in the Heavens, if after all these miracles and wonders, I alone persecute myself more than all our enemies? For I did not overcome my desires, but even welcomed the evil inclination – and then I did what I did, until I brought upon myself all these afflictions; sufferings of the soul that are more difficult and bitter than all sufferings. There is no suffering like the suffering of the soul. Indeed, this is the greatest reason for pity: to extricate a Jewish soul from sins and spiritual damage.

Master of the entire world! Primordial One! God of truth! You alone know the true implication of my words, for I am "empty and know nothing"[8] of the full scope of the miracle of Purim, physically and spiritually – and in particular, how to imbue me with this miracle and deliverance. You alone know all this, and with glimmers of intuition and various hints without measure, You constantly beckon to me from afar as to how I may come closer to You. But I, in my stubbornness, still have not turned back from my straying. Yet this is my consolation in my bitter poverty: that I persist in speaking words such as these before You, and trill my words from the dust unto You, and still hope for Your mercy and deliverance.

Master of the Universe, You alone know the magnitude of the miracle that took place in the days of Mordekhai and Esther, who were privileged to win the war against Haman-Amalek, in order to blot out their name and memory from the world; how, in so doing, they were able to transmit a wondrous illumination and awesome salvation from generation to generation; and how, even now, all our vitality and hope to leave our exile in body and soul can only be found through the power of this miracle. We stand and long for Your deliverance. Just as You helped them in former times to subjugate and destroy the kelipah of Haman-Amalek – to uproot, eradicate and conquer this great force of corruption, to reveal faith in Your Providence to the world, and to return and uphold and receive anew the holiness of Your Torah – so may You come to our aid in every generation until we win the war completely, and utterly wipe out the memory of Amalek. Remove the spirit of impurity from the earth, return us to You in truth, and speedily bring us forth from our bitter exile!

Therefore I have come before You, Master of Wonders, begging You to take to heart the great anguish of our souls. Gaze upon our misery and travail, and do not gaze upon our deeds! Work miracles and wonders for us, "Purim miracles," and set into motion chains of cause and effect for our benefit so that we may return to You during our lifetimes, immediately, without a moment's delay, and never again return to our folly.

Master of the Universe, Who gives life to the living, Living God, Eternal King! Have mercy on us, grant us life, preserve us, sanctify us and purify us from the impurity of contact with the dead, which is the primary source of impurity. This corresponds to immoral thoughts and fantasies, which have come to proliferate throughout the world to the point that "we are drowning in the watery abyss without a foothold; we have entered deep waters, and the rushing current sweeps us away!"[9] Through the power of the holiness of Purim, enable us to receive and imbue ourselves with the holiness and purity of the perfect *Parah Adumah*, which purifies from contact with the dead, both in this world and in the World to Come. And then grant us the merit to receive the holy festival of Pesach, the "season of our liberation,"[10] with great sanctity and immeasurable joy.

In Your mercy, may we merit to fulfill all the mitzvot of Pesach with great holiness, and with great joy and gladness. Protect us from even the smallest amount of chametz and leavening, so that even the least speck of chametz or leavening cannot be found in our domain throughout the days of Pesach. For it is revealed and known to You, Master of the entire world, that it would be impossible for a human being of flesh and blood to be sufficiently vigilant about the least amount of chametz, were it not for Your deliverance and mercy. Have mercy on us in Your abundant compassion, Mighty Redeemer, Truly Merciful One, and guard and save us from even the least amount of chametz throughout the holy days of Pesach. Help us and grant us the privilege to go out "from slavery to freedom, from grief to joy, from mourning to Yom Tov, and from darkness to the greatest light!"[11] Let us celebrate the Pesach Seder with deep fervor, fiery enthusiasm and boundless joy! May we be found worthy of receiving the most wondrous illumination of all states of expanded consciousness and constricted consciousness which shine forth on Pesach with the most awesome, wondrous radiance!

All-Merciful One, help us to fulfill the mitzvot of Purim with such holiness and joy that in this merit we succeed in protecting ourselves from even the least trace of chametz, and fulfill the awesome mitzvot of Pesach with great holiness and profound joy. Have compassion for the sake of Your Name and enable us, even now, to evoke Your mercy. Help us and save us, according to this Torah, to return and draw close to You immediately and truthfully. In the power of the holiness of the miracle and the wondrous deliverance of Purim, save us, so that we may be transformed this very moment from evil to good, and from profuse darkness to great light.

Enable us to complete the Fast of Esther before Purim in great sanctity, to recite the *Selichot* with intense concentration, and to call out and scream to You from the depths. Open my heart, so that I may truly feel the pain of my sins and the profound travail of my soul, which is beyond measure, until I merit to scream a loud and bitter scream, as befits me according to the enormity of my sins and transgressions and the tremendous damage I have done to my soul – until You awaken Your mercies upon me in truth, and hasten to rescue and redeem me from myself, thus to perform "in Your statutes I will walk, and Your mitzvot I will heed,"[12] in truth and with a whole heart.

My Father, my King, my Former, my Creator and my Maker! Teach me the way to begin anew from the holiness of Purim, as You have hinted to us through Your holy sages.[13] Help me in a miraculous manner, through a wondrous deliverance, through a wondrous and awesome innovation, so that from now on I will return to You in complete teshuvah and make a completely new start in serving You with all my heart and soul. Instruct me and teach me how to begin in truth; in which way, and according to which advice, I may return to You.

Master of the Universe, "great in counsel and mighty in deed,"[14] send me good advice and save me quickly for the sake of Your Name, so that I will merit from now on to attain perfect teshuvah all the days of my life, and from this moment on never veer from Your will, "neither to the right or the left."[15] May I merit "to study and teach, to heed, perform and fulfill all the words of Your Torah with love."[16] May I fulfill all mitzvot and all holy tasks, and perform each service in its proper season, and do everything at the appropriate time, with great holiness and purity.

PURIM

Strengthen me with joy and gladness constantly. In the power of the true tzaddikim, may I banish and nullify from me and from all Israel the kelipah of Haman-Amalek, may their names be blotted out; and may I draw upon myself the holiness of the miracle and deliverance of Purim. Have mercy on us in every generation and in every year, that we should be privileged to rejoice greatly during the days of Purim with the greatest delight, and that we may fulfill the mitzvot of reading the Megillah in great holiness and purity and boundless joy. May we contemplate this awesome miracle and astounding redemption, and publicize the miracle to every person and assemblage.

Grant us the privilege of fulfilling the mitzvot of sending foods (*mishlo'ach manot*) to our friends and neighbors, giving charity to the poor, and celebrating the festive meal in honor of Purim, wholeheartedly and with great joy.

Enable us to fulfill the mitzvah of drinking to the point of intoxication on Purim, as our sages of blessed memory have instructed us,[17] and help us and protect us so that absolutely no harm befalls us from drinking on Purim, neither physical nor spiritual, and no harm befalls any person or property as a result of our drinking. Rather, let us attain only the greatest joy and delight through drinking on Purim. May we experience the true joy of Purim, when an awesome spiritual illumination shines on us – the light of Mordekhai, the likes of which cannot be glimpsed at any other time of year. Let us rejoice with all our hearts and gladden the hearts of others, and cause all Israel to rejoice with the joy of Purim in absolute ecstasy! Let us delight and exult in Your salvation with true joy, in a manner that You will find gratifying, favorable and a source of pleasure, due to our drinking and celebrating on Purim.

Even now, may we be privy to the great miracle and wondrous deliverance of Purim every year, and may we subjugate, uproot and eradicate from our midst the kelipah of Haman-Amalek and its tremendous corruption, and blot out its name and memory from the world. Help us to cleanse ourselves of this corruption with the greatest sanctity and purification, and imbue ourselves with the holiness of Mordekhai and Esther.

May we transmit the joy of Purim to the rest of the year entirely, and rejoice in You constantly with the greatest delight. Through this, may we be privy to the holiness of the *Parah Adumah* and the holiness of Pesach, and be happy always. Fulfill in us the words of the verse: "For in Him our hearts will rejoice, for in His holy Name we trusted."[18] "May the words of my mouth and the meditation of my heart be acceptable before You, my Rock and my Redeemer."[19]

(LT II, 37)

Notes

1 See p 89, note 2.
2 See Numbers 19.
3 Although the public reading of the Torah passage about the *Parah Adumah* on the Shabbat after Purim does not confer actual ritual purity, it has a spiritual effect, enabling us to commemorate the offering of the *Korban Pesach* with sincere devotion. According to the Kabbalists, these two rituals also effect tikkunim that benefit the supernal worlds and even the physical world of our ordinary experience.

4 *Midrash Mishlei* 9:2.
5 *Likutey Moharan* II, 74. Reb Noson writes that although Rebbe Nachman did not finish this sentence, he nevertheless indicated that today all "beginnings" stem from Purim, since at that time the Jews waged war against Haman-Amalek, which represents the antithesis of faith; see Rabbi Noson Zvi Koenig, *Torat Natan al Likutey Moharan*, ad loc., sec. 5, citing *Likutey Halakhot*; also cf. Rabbi Avraham b'Reb Nachman, *Kokhavey Ohr, Chokhmah U'Binah*, sec. 47, s.v. *Geulah HaRishonah*. The Hebrew word *Amalek* has the same numerical value as *safek* (doubt). Our great challenge today is to remain firm in our faith against all doubts and confusions.
6 Pesach Haggadah.
7 "Haman-Amalek" refers to a kelipah (unholy force) rather than two of the historical enemies of the Jewish people. This kelipah stands in opposition to faith, and will be destroyed at the End of Days.
8 Paraphrase of Psalms 73:22.
9 Paraphrase of Psalms 69:3.
10 Liturgy.
11 Pesach Haggadah.
12 Paraphrase of Leviticus 26:3.
13 *Likutey Moharan* II, 74.
14 Jeremiah 32:19.
15 Paraphrase of Deuteronomy 17:11. In Kabbalistic terminology, the "right" represents the attribute of Chesed (Kindness), while the "left" represents the attribute of Gevurah (Judgment).
16 Liturgy, *Birkat Kri'at Shma*.
17 The Talmud (*Megillah* 7a) declares: "A person is obligated to drink on Purim until he no longer can distinguish between 'Cursed is Haman' and 'Blessed is Mordekhai'" Cf. *Shulchan Arukh, Orach Chaim* 695:2; Rabbi Chaim Vital, *Sha'ar HaKavanot*, 104a. However, one may fulfill this mitzvah by drinking more wine than usual and taking a nap; see gloss of Rema, *Orach Chaim* 695:2, citing Maharil; *Sha'arei Teshuvah*, s.v. *veyishan*; et al. A person who may not drink alcohol for medical reasons is entirely exempt. In Breslov tradition, Purim is the only day of the year

when it is customary to become intoxicated. One does so during the course of the Purim feast, after having performed all the other mitzvot of the day.
18 Psalms 33:21.
19 Psalms 19:15.

61

Banishing Haman, Crowning Mordekhai

Lust for money leads people to commit all kinds of sins that tarnish their souls and strengthen the kelipah of Haman-Amalek. If only we were to hearken to Mordekhai and Esther, we would understand the real value of gold and silver.

Have mercy and save us from the lust for wealth. Help us to break the craving for social status and riches, and may we not harbor the least desire to accumulate wealth in this world that does not belong to us. Rather, let our entire passion, longing and striving be for the holy Torah – to acquire wisdom and Divine knowledge, and to cleave to Your holy mitzvot.

Grant us the merit of fixing in our lifetimes all the damage we have caused through the desire for wealth. May we redeem all the sparks of holiness that the kelipah devoured, due to our many sins and the evil passions that led us to commit them – especially our craving for money. Speedily fulfill the verse: "He devoured wealth, but will disgorge it; God will purge it from his gut."[1] May we overcome, destroy, nullify, eradicate, annihilate and uproot the kelipah of Haman-Amalek[2] from the world – this being the lust for wealth. May we extricate the holy life force from this kelipah and restore all the lost sparks of holiness and vitality to their supernal source, and transform them into Torah.

Enable us to draw upon ourselves constantly the holiness of Mordekhai and Esther. Help us to reveal and

ENTERING THE LIGHT

cause to shine all the sublime colors inherent in silver, gold and copper, in great sanctity and purity, according to Your beneficent will. Have compassion toward us, in Your abundant mercy, and confer upon us the trait of true compassion. So may we show compassion toward all creatures, and perform many acts of charity and kindness.

(*Tefilot VeTachanunim* I, *Tefilah* 56)

Notes
1. Job 20:15.
2. "Haman-Amalek" refers to a kelipah (unholy force) rather than two of the historical enemies of the Jewish people. This kelipah stands in opposition to faith, and will be destroyed at the End of Days.

Shalosh Regalim
The Three Pilgrim Festivals

62

Raising Up the Shekhinah

On Pesach, Shavuot and Sukkot, we rejoice with delicious food, fine wine, new clothes and a respite from work. And we pray to come even closer to the essence of Yom Tov by elevating the Shekhinah to the Light of God's Face.

In Your abundant mercy and immense kindness, help me to receive the Three Pilgrim Festivals (Pesach, Shavuot and Sukkot) with great holiness and profound joy. Enable me to honor all the Pilgrim Festivals and holidays with much honor and grandeur, with fine food and drink and clean garments, by desisting from mundane work, with a good heart and great joy, with intense prayer and spiritual arousal, as is befitting on the holy Yom Tov.

Grant me the privilege of performing many mitzvot throughout the year, in great holiness and joy; and may the joy of the mitzvot of the entire year gather together and flow into the "heart" of the year, which is composed of the Three Pilgrim Festivals. Thus I will attain the true joy of Yom Tov, as it is written: "You shall rejoice on your festival."[1]

May I rejoice with the greatest ecstasy on all Three Pilgrim Festivals. As it is written: "We shall sing and rejoice in You"[2] for having chosen us from all nations and elevating us from all languages, until we merit to ascend and "see and be seen"[3] in the Light of God's Face.

Help us to fulfill all the mitzvot related to each festival, so that we may elevate the Shekhinah, which is represented by the number four, to the Light of the Face. These mitzvot are: on Pesach, the Four Cups; on Shavuot, the Receiving of the Torah (which Moses taught four times and the Jews learned four times in the wilderness);[4] and on Sukkot, the Four Species.

Please, God, have mercy on us and grant us the privilege of truly fulfilling to perfection all these awesome mitzvot in their time and season on each festival, together with all other awesome and holy mitzvot pertaining to each festival. May we fulfill them completely, with the greatest joy and gladness, with awe and love, until we elevate the holy aspect of Malkhut to the Light of the Face that shines on the Three Pilgrim Festivals.

May I return to You in perfect teshuvah because of joy on all these days. Be gracious to me, in Your great mercy, so that I will repent even for those sins that remain unknown to me!

Master of the Universe! You know how far I am from the holiness and joy of Yom Tov! Have pity on me, in Your abundant mercy and profound kindness, and allow me to receive the holidays with great holiness and joy, until I succeed in liberating the holy aspect of Malkhut from the dominion of the Four Kingdoms of Evil, and elevate Her to the Light of God's Face, in fulfillment of the verse: "Justice will walk before Him, and He will set His footsteps upon the way."[5] And it states: "Surely the tzaddikim will give thanks to Your Name; the upright will dwell before Your Face!"[6]

Let me draw upon myself the holiness and joy of Yom Tov throughout the entire year and be happy always, until I am worthy of attaining intuitions of Your Godliness, perceptions of Your exaltedness and yearnings of faith, sincerely and wholeheartedly, with joy and beneficence, with great holiness and purity!

Have mercy on us and send us our righteous Redeemer speedily in our days, and fulfill the verse: "As in the days of your Exodus from Egypt, I will show you wonders."[7]

Grant me the privilege of immediately ascending, beholding and prostrating myself before You in our Holy Temple three times a year on the Pilgrim Festivals!

(LT I, 30)

Notes
1. Deuteronomy 16:14.
2. Song of Songs 1:4.
3. *Chagigah* 4b.
4. See *Eruvin* 54b.
5. Psalms 85:14.
6. Psalms 140:14.
7. Micah 7:15.

63

Seeing the Light of Yom Tov

Since the tzaddikim establish the calendar and, by extension, the festivals, and the Talmud states that it is a mitzvah to "receive the face of one's teacher on the festival,"[1] Rebbe Nachman infers that the tzaddikim are a channel for the spiritual light of Yom Tov (Likutey Moharan I, 135). That spiritual light can be ours, too, when we welcome each Yom Tov with honor, joy and a magnanimous heart – and attach ourselves to a true tzaddik.

O God and God of our fathers, in Your abundant mercy and profound kindness, allow me to greet all the festivals in great holiness and purity, with joy, gladness and a magnanimous heart, to the ultimate degree, according to Your beneficent will.

Grant me the privilege of receiving the light of my teacher's face on the festival, even when I am physically distant from him. May I be worthy to receive the light of the faces of the true tzaddikim – to perceive them, and to love them, and to draw their holiness upon myself by virtue of greeting the festival; for the sanctity of the festivals is drawn from them.

May I attain the Forty-Nine Gates of Understanding that are revealed and shine forth on the holy Yom Tov. Open for me the light of holy intellect, and may I truly engage in deep contemplation of Your Torah and Your service. Thus may I eradicate all foolishness from within me – all forms of pride, self-importance and conceit; and may I attain the ultimate degree of humility, according to Your beneficent will.

ENTERING THE LIGHT

Constantly draw upon me and upon all Israel the holiness of Moses our teacher, peace be upon him. He entered all Forty-Nine Gates of Understanding and so attained true humility. As it is written: "And the man Moses was extremely humble, more than anyone on the face of the earth."[2]

Have mercy on us, God full of mercy, that in the power of welcoming the festivals, "seasons of God, holy convocations,"[3] we may imbue ourselves with the holiness of Moses our teacher and the holiness of all true tzaddikim. Through them, may we draw upon ourselves all higher perceptions and holy true insights which are drawn from Yom Tov. Help us to drive away all forms of self-importance, arrogance and egotistic bias until we attain true humility – the humility of Moses our teacher.

(LT I, 99)

Notes
1 *Sukkah* 27b.
2 Numbers 12:3.
3 Liturgy, *Shalosh Regalim Kiddush*.

64

"Serve God with Joy"

Our rejoicing on the festivals can reach all the way to the Heavens, elevating "fallen joys" and bringing us closer to the ultimate joy of God's deliverance.

Master of the Universe! Protect me and save me, so that I may never damage the joy of the holy festivals. Enable me to rejoice in holy ecstasy on every festival, "seasons of God, holy convocations."[1] May I fulfill the mitzvah of "You shall rejoice on your holiday"[2] to the fullest, with all its details, fine points and intentions, as well as the complete structure of 613 mitzvot that depend on it.[3]

Guard my soul and save me from belittling the festivals. Have mercy on me and on all Israel, and do not let us be included among those who belittle the festivals – those about whom our sages state that they forfeit their place in the World to Come, being tantamount to idolaters.[4]

Save me from the shame and disgrace that come from disparaging the festivals, God forbid. Be with me always, and protect me and save me that "my foot should not falter."[5] "Do not allow my foot to slip"[6] so that I should not lose my balance, or ever let myself slip and fall, physically or spiritually. And may others not rejoice in my downfall, God forbid, or make a laughingstock of me.

Fulfill the verse: "He set my feet upon a rock, firmly establishing my steps."[7] Encourage and strengthen me in Your wondrous ways, so that I may always experience the joy of the festivals to the fullest. "Shine Your Face upon Your servant, save me in Your kindness."[8] Let me rejoice on every festival, and celebrate with all my might, and feel the joy of Yom Tov in my heart!

All-Merciful One, Joy of Israel! Instill joy in my heart, especially on the holy and awesome festivals, so that I will "sing and rejoice in You."[9] Have mercy on me, and forgive me for all the ways I have been remiss in rejoicing on Yom Tov, past and present. Help me to fix everything completely by elevating all the "fallen joys" to their proper station and spiritual source – to the place where their transcendent lights[10] originally shone forth. Allow me to become familiar with all the ways of joy, so that I will always be happy, especially on Shabbat and festivals, and sing and rejoice in Your deliverance.

"O Lord our God, grant us as our inheritance, in joy and gladness, Your holy seasons; and Israel will rejoice in You, those who sanctify Your Name!"[11]

(LT I, 140)

Notes

1 Liturgy, *Shalosh Regalim Kiddush*.
2 Deuteronomy 16:14.
3 See p. 89, note 2.
4 *Pesachim* 118a. Rebbe Nachman discusses this axiom in *Likutey Moharan* I, 14:10 and 235.
5 Paraphrase of Psalms 37:31.
6 Paraphrase of Psalms 121:3.
7 Psalms 40:3.
8 Psalms 31:17.
9 Song of Songs 1:4.

10 Reb Noson uses the term *ohalam* (their tents). We have rendered this interpretively as an allusion to the *ohr makif* (transcendent light), the Heavenly repository of joy.
11 Liturgy, Yom Tov *Shemoneh Esrei*.

65

Eradicating the Three Cravings

The Divine perceptions we gain on the Three Pilgrim Festivals enable us to combat the destructive influence of the three evil lusts: the cravings for wealth, sexual pleasure and tasty foods.

In Your abundant mercy, enable us to receive the Three Pilgrim Festivals of Pesach, Shavuot and Sukkot with great joy and gladness, with holy fear and love, and with the utmost purity, according to Your beneficent will. Let us honor them with every sort of honor and delight – with fine food and drink, with honorable clothing, with sincere prayer, and with great joy and spiritual arousal.

May we draw new perceptions of Godliness on each of the Three Pilgrim Festivals, and renew the three "mentalities" that are found in the three cavities of the skull, which are Chokhmah, Binah and Da'at. Thus may we utterly eradicate all three evil lusts: the cravings for wealth, sexual pleasure and tasty foods. These cravings are the source of our troubles, and through them we have lost what we have lost, and come to what we have come to.

Please, God, have mercy on us, have pity on our souls, have pity on our children and infants, have pity on us and on all who depend on us. Have pity on Your glory! Confer merit upon us from now on, encourage and strengthen us, gladden us with holy joy, and transmit to us great and holy inner power until we speedily eradicate all three lusts. Through the holiness of the Three Pilgrim Festivals, may we imbue our hearts with Divine perception. In this way, may we spiritually rectify our hearts and nullify these three lusts to the point that no trace of them remains at all.

Grant us the merit of receiving in holiness the holiday of Pesach, the time of our liberation, and in so doing elicit the mentality and higher perception to destroy the craving for wealth. In the merit of the holiday of Shavuot, may we draw the mentality and higher perception to destroy the craving for sexual pleasure. And in the merit of the holiday of Sukkot, the harvest festival, may we elicit the mentality and higher perception to destroy the craving for tasty foods.

Please, God, make known to us Your ways so that we may know how to find favor in Your sight, and how to succeed in presenting our entreaties before You – so that we may draw close to You in truth and fulfill all the good advice that we have received from Your true tzaddikim. Then we will be able to return to You completely, with a whole heart.

In Your great compassion, confer upon us merit and grace so that we all may be privileged to greet the Three Pilgrim Festivals with boundless joy and gladness. Instill in us the true joy of Yom Tov! Have pity on us, for we do not know any other way to attain the joy of Yom Tov, except through Your power alone.

"Sanctify us with Your mitzvot and grant us our portion in Your Torah. Satisfy us with Your goodness, gladden us with Your deliverance, and purify our hearts to serve You in truth. O Lord our God, grant us as our inheritance, in joy and gladness, Your holy seasons,"[1] until in the merit of the Three Pilgrim Festivals, we succeed in eradicating the three evil lusts – the cravings for wealth, sexual pleasure and tasty foods. May we truly become holy and pure.

Take us out of darkness and bring us into light! May we merit to draw forth Divine perception and instill it in our hearts, thus to correct and purify the heart from all three cravings. Fulfill in us the verse: "And you shall know this day and place it upon your heart that the Lord is God; in heaven above and on earth below, there is none other!"[2]

(LT II, 1)

Notes

1. Liturgy, Yom Tov *Shemoneh Esrei*.
2. Deuteronomy 4:39. Reb Noson expounds on the mystical implications of this verse in *Likutey Halakhot, Choshen Mishpat, Shekhiv MeyRa* 2:2.

Nisan

66

Magnetic Pull

With apt imagery, Reb Noson characterizes the true tzaddikim as the gravitational force that draws others close to God, and those who oppose holiness as the repelling force that pulls the Jewish people away from their Creator. With prayer, we can enlist God's help to swing the battle in the right direction.

"Draw me close (*MaShKheiNi*) – after You we shall hasten!"[1]

Your great and holy glory, arouse and awaken!

Master of the Universe! Glorious King, Whose glory fills the entire universe! Through Your abundant kindness, You gave us true tzaddikim in every generation, with whom Your glory resides. And in Your great mercy, You made known to us that there is no orphaned generation. Even in these generations, You have shown us wondrous kindnesses and given us great and awesome, true tzaddikim. Holy and awesome are their names, for all holy glory resides with them! They are the *MiShKaN* of Your glory, upon whom the holiness of Godliness is drawn forth and rests constantly. For they are truly humble, making themselves as the dust upon which the entire panorama of Creation stands; and everything is drawn from them.

These tzaddikim are the "foundations of the world,"[2] the very foundation of all Creation, and all beings need to draw near to them, to receive their life and continued existence from them. Upon them everything stands, and all Jewish souls are "branches" extending from them and drawn toward them, receiving all life and bounty from them. For they give life to all, and possess the "gravitational force" to draw Godliness to them, and to draw all humanity to them – to bring them all near to You, may You be blessed forever!

Master of the Universe! Master of the Universe! Lord, God of truth! You know these true tzaddikim who possess this power. You know their greatness, their strength, their beauty and their enduring might, as well as the tremendous power they possess to pull the entire world to themselves, to their holy teachings, and to their wondrous ways and advice. How much everlasting benefit has already sprouted forth from them! The tikkun of all the worlds and the Complete Redemption that is destined to come all depend on this – for the arrival of the Mashiach depends on our coming close to the tzaddikim. Yet You know, Master of the entire world, the vast array of forces amassed against us that strive with all their might to tear us away and distance us from the tzaddikim – for the "repelling force" constantly fortifies itself to create a rift and estrange us from the tzaddikim.

Master of the Universe! Lord, God, Who fights our battles! Lofty and Holy One, Who performs mighty deeds in constantly new ways! Mighty One, Who wages our wars! You know the fierce and awesome battle that goes on constantly, from generation to generation, between the gravitational force of the true tzaddikim – who possess the ability to draw the entire world to themselves in order to bring us closer to the Creator, may His Name be blessed forever – and the repelling force that continually fortifies itself against the gravitational force in order to cut us off and distance us both from the tzaddikim and from God. How many souls have fallen in this war and lost both worlds, due to the repelling force that estranged them from the true tzaddikim! And as for us, "orphans of orphans,"[3] what has taken place and what can be done? Who will wage war on our behalf, to conquer and destroy the repelling force that opposes the gravitational force of the tzaddikim?

Master of the Universe! "O God, the mighty and strong, O God, strong in battle!"[4] We cast our burden upon You, so that You will battle for us! O God, "take up our fight and wage our war,"[5] for "You are exalted forever, O God,"[6] and "forever Your Hand is uppermost!"[7]

Have mercy on us and save us in the merit of the true tzaddikim, who possess the gravitational force – and enable the gravitational force to muster its strength to such a great and awesome degree that it will overcome and utterly defeat the repelling force that seeks to cut us off from the tzaddikim and from God. All the obstacles, estrangements, tricks to divert and thwart us, doubts, and all the various disputes and thorny questions, as well as all evil desires and traits, all barriers in the world – they all come from the repelling force. Make them all fall away and vanish completely before the power of the gravitational force of the true tzaddikim, until we and our children and all the Children of Israel – indeed, all creatures in the world – are brought close to the true tzaddikim. Then "they will cast away their false gods of silver and gold"[8] and all their passions in order to follow and run after the true tzaddikim. May we all merit to draw near to the true tzaddikim with the greatest closeness, and hear their holy teachings, study their holy books, and completely fulfill all their holy words, advice and even casual remarks, in truth and simplicity – until we return to You in perfect teshuvah, speedily, sincerely and wholeheartedly, "with joy and with a good heart from the abundance of everything!"[9]

Enable us to destroy and nullify all evil desires and evil traits. May we succeed in nullifying the ego entirely, to the point that we attain true humility and embody the paradigm of the "dust of the earth." Then we too will possess the gravitational force and draw down Your Godliness and holiness upon us. In this way, we will bring the entire world to Your holy faith, Your true tzaddikim, Your service and Your holy Torah, which You revealed to us through Moses, Your prophet, and through all true tzaddikim of every generation.

In Your great mercy, give us the privilege of contributing tzedakah generously to worthy people in need, particularly the true tzaddikim and their children.[10] Help us to give them tzedakah with the greatest honor and respect, and provide for all their needs with dignity. May we give all our charitable contributions to true tzaddikim who are truly humble, exemplifying the paradigm of dust; and through this may our tzedakah produce "fruit" immediately, as it is written: "Sow for yourselves righteousness (*tzedakah*), and reap according to [God's] kindness."[11] Through tzedakah, cause all goodness to sprout forth – "goodly bounty and blessing, compassion, life and peace,"[12] "children, life and sustenance,"[13] and all good things forever!

In Your great mercy, protect us and save us so that we may never stumble because of unworthy poor people. May none of our charity be distributed to an undeserving person whose life is devoted to destroying Your world and not to improving it.¹⁴ Rather, may we give charity generously to worthy poor people and to true tzaddikim. Help us for the sake of Your Name, have pity on us in Your abundant mercy, and enable us to attain all this right away!

Help us to flee from honor to the utmost degree. Instead, may we draw upon ourselves glory from the side of holiness for the sake of Your Name – glory drawn from the true tzaddik, who possesses the gravitational force by which he erects the Mishkan constantly. All sacred honor rests with him, and all elders of Israel, leaders and officers, from the greatest to the smallest, receive their honor from him.

Grant us this kind of sacred honor through which Your great glory will be revealed, magnified and sanctified in the world, constantly. "Rule over the entire world in Your glory"¹⁵ speedily, and let Your glory fill all the earth. As it is written: "Declare among the nations His glory; among all peoples His wonders. They shall recount the glory of Your dominion, and they shall speak of Your might. Blessed is the Lord, God of Israel, Who alone performs wonders! May the name of His glory be blessed forever, and may His glory fill all the earth. Amen!"¹⁶

(LT I, 70)

Notes

1. Song of Songs 1:4.
2. Paraphrase of Proverbs 10:25.
3. *Ketuvot* 106a.
4. Psalms 24:8.
5. Liturgy, *Shemoneh Esrei*.

6 Psalms 92:9.
7 *Vayikra Rabbah* 24:2; also cf. Rashi on Psalms 92:9.
8 Paraphrase of Isaiah 2:20.
9 Deuteronomy 28:47.
10 The priorities of giving charity are delineated in *Shulchan Arukh, Yoreh De'ah* 247-259.
11 Hosea 10:12.
12 Liturgy, *Shemoneh Esrei*.
13 *Mo'ed Katan* 28a.
14 According to the *Shulchan Arukh, Yoreh De'ah* 251:1, one is exempt from giving charity to an unrepentant, willful sinner of Israel. However, we are obligated to give charity to the poor of our people as well as to poor non-Jews, for this promotes peace. In a broader sense, Rabbi Pinchas Eliyahu Horowitz of Vilna, an eighteenth-century Kabbalist, states: "Love of one's neighbor means that we should love all people, no matter to which nation they belong or which language they speak. For all men are created in the Divine image, and all engage in improving civilization. ... However, excluded from this love are those who willfully destroy civilization, such as murderers, thieves and pirates" (see *Sefer HaBrit* II, Discourse 13, *Ma'amar Ahavat Rei'a*).
15 Liturgy, Rosh HaShanah.
16 Liturgy, Daily Prayers.

67

Season of Our Liberation

Just as the month of Nisan heralded the redemption of the Jewish people in days of old, it can herald each Jew's personal redemption in our days.

Help us to draw forth the holiness of the month of Nisan, the "first of months,"[1] upon ourselves and all Israel. Just as You brought forth Your nation, Israel, from exile in Egypt, the "lewdness of the earth,"[2] at this season, so may You mercifully redeem every soul of Your people, Israel, in every year and every generation. Save us all through the power of this holy month of Nisan, the first of months, during which You brought about the redemption and salvation of Israel – and through this, may we all experience our own personal redemption. Free our souls without delay from the abyss of destruction, from the spiritual quagmire, and deliver us from the depths of the sea!

Save our wretched souls from the spiritual damage of nocturnal emissions, God forbid, and may we never succumb to this transgression – neither us nor our offspring, nor the offspring of any one of Your people, the House of Israel, now and forever.

Our Father, our King, have mercy on us! Our Father, our King, have mercy on us and on our infants and children, and enable us to draw forth the holiness and joy of the month of Nisan and transmit it to the rest of the year. Let us always be joyous, and constantly bring joy, gladness, strength and mirth to all the holy angels. Let there be splendor and majesty before them, "might and gladness in their place"[3] throughout the entire year, just as during the month of Nisan!

Grant us the merit to give strength and vigor to the holy angels through our rejoicing, and may the holy angels be fortified constantly with all power and might. May we nullify the power of the demons and kelipot, and not give them any nurture from the holy *shefa* that descends to us, so that our food and drink will be spiritually refined, and we will be saved from the pollution of nocturnal emissions, and always remain holy and pure.

(LT II, 5)

Notes

1 The first day of Nisan is designated as the "Rosh HaShanah for kings," since each year of a Jewish monarch's reign is counted from that day; see *Mishnah Rosh HaShanah* 2a.
2 Genesis 42:9.
3 Paraphrase of I Chronicles 16:27.

Shabbat HaGadol

The Shabbat Before Pesach

68

Perceiving Divine Providence

The Author of Creation maintains an active presence in the lives of every one of His creatures. Here is a prayer for greater awareness of God's role in our lives.

Master of the Universe! Grant me the trait of holy alacrity, so that I never become lazy in the performance of any mitzvah, God forbid. Rather, may I fulfill all the words of Your Torah and Your mitzvot with eagerness, and not pay attention to worries about livelihood. May I believe that You will surely sustain me, and the God Who watched over me until now like a shepherd will not abandon me. Through my alacrity, may my mind and soul be energized, and may I minimize the time wasted in sleep due to laziness. Instead, may I always serve You diligently and enthusiastically, and whenever it is possible to snatch a bit of Torah, or perform a mitzvah, may I do so right away, without any procrastination or laziness.

Imbue in me the realization that time does exist – for the essence of Divine Providence lies in knowing that God transcends time and space, and that He watches over the entire universe through His Providence, and what we take to be nature is an illusion. Help us to attain higher consciousness and awareness, and through our faith, may we be privileged to have You relate to us in wondrous and miraculous ways, utterly beyond the laws of nature. Let us draw the full manifestation of Your Divine Providence from the spiritual plane known as the World to Come.

SHABBAT HAGADOL

Let us receive Shabbat in a joyous frame of mind, "with wealth and honor, and with few mistakes."[1] For everything is drawn through the holiness of Shabbat – by virtue of our belief that God created all the worlds, bringing them into being *yesh me'ayin* (something from nothing), and that everything reflects Divine Providence, and that nature has no autonomy whatsoever – since we know that the laws of nature, too, operate according to Divine Providence. And we believe in all the miracles that You performed for us and for our patriarchs, Abraham, Isaac and Jacob, truly believing in all of them. And we remind ourselves of our Exodus from Egypt every day, in order to enlighten our minds with the realization that everything reflects Divine Providence.

May I be privileged to receive the holiness of Shabbat HaGadol, which immediately precedes the holiday of Pesach. In the merit of this day, may You put an end to all our sufferings, destroy our oppressors, and eradicate evil forever!

(Tefilot HaBoker, Tefilah 7)

Notes

1 Paraphrase of prayer recited by some after *Shalom Aleikhem.*

69

Holy Fire

Only with God's help can we search out and burn all the chametz in our possession on Erev Pesach, and avoid chametz completely during the holiday. And only with prayer can we nullify the harsh judgments and evil which threaten to consume us with their unholy fire.

May it be Your will, Lord our God, to perform miracles and wonders for us in fulfillment of the verse: "As in the days of your Exodus from Egypt, I will show you wonders!"[1]

Protect us from all harmful forces; may they be deprived of any ability to damage us physically or spiritually. Save us from all forms of darkness, and shine upon us a glimmer of Your holy Light, from which all other lights – both physical and spiritual – derive. Enable us to transmit the holiness of Pesach night[2] to the entire year, and thereby be protected from all darkness and harmful forces, as well as from all afflictions and harsh judgments which might overpower us due to our many sins and transgressions. Illuminate us with Your Infinite Light and fulfill in us the verse: "And [the darkness of] night shines like [the light of] the day!"[3] Watch over us with Your Providence, and remove all harm and harsh judgments from us and from Your entire nation, Israel, forever.

Each year, allow us to nullify the chametz from our homes and domains on the day before Pesach.[4] By burning the chametz, may we eradicate all idolatry and evil from the world, in fulfillment of the verse: "For they came forth from the fire, and the fire shall consume them."[5]

Subjugate the "Luminaries of Fire" and reveal and strengthen the holiness of the "Luminaries of Light." The latter are the true tzaddikim who reveal Divine Providence to the world, and who subjugate and cancel all harsh judgments produced by the Luminaries of Fire, which are bound up with nature. You have already made known to us through Your true tzaddikim that the power of nature is drawn primarily from the paradigm of fire, which represents the full force of harsh judgment. The attitude of a person who declares, "My power and the strength of my hand [made for me this wealth],"[6] God forbid, is elicited from the power of fire, which was created on Motza'ei Shabbat (Saturday night) by Adam, as our sages of blessed memory declare.[7] Thus, the power of nature derives from fire. However, in truth, nature itself reflects Your beneficent Providence. Our main task is to incorporate nature into Your Providence, and in so doing, restore the paradigm of fire to the holy. Then we will perform all the commandments with the warmth of holy fire that consumes all fires from the Other Side.

Then all idolatry and evil will be nullified and fall away, and we will merit to perform the ceremony of havdalah every Motza'ei Shabbat, and recite the blessing over fire. All harsh judgments will be nullified, as well as the Other Side and all idolatry, in fulfillment of the verse: "And the House of Jacob will be a fire; and the House of Joseph, a flame; and the House of Esau for straw."[8] They will be nullified and consumed by the fire of holiness.

We will attain all this by burning the chametz every Erev Pesach. Then we will merit to eat the matzah in holiness and reveal Divine Providence, as we declare during the Pesach Seder: "We eat this matzah because the dough of our forefathers did not have time to rise before the Supreme King of kings, the Holy One, blessed be He, was revealed to them, and redeemed them!"[9]

Master of the Universe! You know that it is impossible for human beings of flesh and blood to be truly on guard against even the least speck of chametz throughout the days of Pesach. It is only because You watch over us in Your great kindness that we can succeed in our vigilance concerning the least speck of chametz throughout the days of Pesach. By remaining steadfast in not eating chametz, we will nullify the illusion of nature completely, remove from ourselves all harsh judgments, and eat matzah in holiness and purity. Then we will attain true knowledge of God and bring down a full manifestation of Providence upon ourselves and upon all Israel. By eating matzah during the seven days of Pesach, we will imbue ourselves with the holiness of the Exodus from Egypt every year. More Divine Providence will be revealed until we realize that nature, too, operates according to Your beneficent Providence, and the natural order has no autonomous existence.

As a result, materialist philosophy will be refuted and negated along with the Other Side and all forms of idolatry to which it gives rise. All enemies and antagonists will be put to shame. We will witness miracles and believe in Your miracles: the Exodus from Egypt and the crossing of the Red Sea. We will know that all this came about because You revealed Your Unity and Oneness in the world, and we will perceive that everything operates according to Divine Providence, utterly beyond the laws of nature.

SHABBAT HAGADOL

Then, after Pesach, we will be able to eat even chametz – for it will have been revealed that nature, which is an aspect of chametz, is entirely a manifestation of Your Providence alone. This is the essence of higher consciousness, which nullifies all sufferings and harsh judgments and brings about the downfall of all evil regimes that dominate us in our exile. The "two tears" will fall into the Great Sea[10] and put an end to the wicked, while accomplishing miracles for our good.

We will sing a new song of thanksgiving to You for our redemption and the liberation of our souls – a song of Providence, a song of wonders and miracles. "From God this came about; it is wondrous in our sight!"[11]

May we be privileged to drink the Four Cups on Pesach night in holiness and purity, and elevate our minds in sanctity, until we depart from foolish consciousness, impoverished consciousness. Through our drinking in holiness, may we merit to tell the story of the Exodus from Egypt all the days of our lives, in fulfillment of the verse: "In order that you remember the day of your Exodus from the land of Egypt, all the days of your lives."[12]

Let us thank and praise Your great Name for the miracles and wonders that You performed for us in the past, and which You will perform for us in the future. By drinking the Four Cups, may we banish sleep and the lack of higher consciousness, which is compared to sleep, and nullify all poverty and oppression, both physical and spiritual. May we be worthy of "wine that brings joy to God and man,"[13] and speak holy words and sing songs and praises that arise from sublime perception.

Reveal Your Providence over us, abolish the darkness, and grant us light until the "night shines like the day."[14]

Correct the deficiency of the moon, and "may the light of the moon be like the light of the sun."[15] Remove all poverty and lack from our midst, and elevate our minds until we merit to speak holy words, in fulfillment of the verse: "And your palate is like vintage wine; it goes to my Beloved in righteousness, causing the lips of sleepers to speak."[16] Thus we will open our mouths in holiness, and we will sing, exalt and praise You constantly.

(*Tefilot HaBoker, Tefilah* 7)

Notes

1 Micah 7:15.
2 That is, the night of the Seder.
3 Psalms 139:12.
4 The laws and customs of searching for the chametz on the night before Pesach, and burning it and nullifying it the following morning, are detailed in *Shulchan Arukh, Orach Chaim* 431-445. Today, it is customary to nullify chametz in all three ways: by verbally renouncing it, by destroying it, and by selling it, usually through one's local Orthodox rabbi.
5 Ezekiel 15:7.
6 Deuteronomy 8:17.
7 *Bereshit Rabbah* 11:2.
8 Obadiah 1:18.
9 Pesach Haggadah.
10 The Talmud states: "What is an earthquake? At the time God remembers that His children are living in suffering among the nations, He sheds two tears into the Great Sea, and His voice is heard from one end of the world to the other" (*Berakhot* 59a). These two tears represent the arousal of God's compassion for His people, and the subsequent vengeance He will exact from the nations that persecuted the Jewish people.
11 Psalms 118:23.

12 Deuteronomy 16:3.
13 Paraphrase of Judges 9:13.
14 Psalms 139:12.
15 Paraphrase of liturgy, *Kiddush Levanah*; cf. Isaiah 30:26.
16 Song of Songs 7:10.

Pesach

70

Pesach Preparations

On Seder night, we try to envision ourselves as slaves in Egypt and thank God for having redeemed us as well. To reach such a level of awareness, we beg God to let us experience our freedom to the ultimate degree.

O God, help us to take upon ourselves the sanctity of Pesach with awesome holiness and great joy and gladness. May we fulfill the mitzvah of drinking the Four Cups during the Pesach Seder meal properly, in great holiness and purity. Disclose to us the light of Divine perception, and pour forth upon us the light of the various sublime states of mind, so that we should be privileged to receive on Pesach all holy levels of higher perception – expanded consciousness and constricted consciousness.[1]

May we perform the Pesach Seder in great sanctity, as is befitting. Enable us to recite the Haggadah in a strong voice, with intense and awesome concentration, with profound joy and gladness, with deep fervor and fiery passion, and with holiness and purity, until our voices awaken the intention of the heart. Then we will attain the tikkun of the covenant and tikkun of the mind to the ultimate degree, and receive new Torah insights, in truth.

(LT I, 20)

Notes

1 See Rabbi Chaim Vital, *Pri Etz Chaim, Sha'ar Chag HaMatzot* 1.

71

Purging the Heart of Chametz

We would all be loyal, loving servants of God were it not for the "chametz in the dough" that leads us astray with dreams of glory and power. Help us, God, to weed out and nullify this "chametz" so that we can return to You in truth.

Master of the Universe, "Who gives a voice to the mute,"[1] give us a voice with which to speak words of Your Torah and relate Your true wonders constantly, "in order that the last generation may know; children yet to be born will arise and tell their children."[2] May we merit to make known to our children and grandchildren, as well as to all the Children of Israel throughout their generations, all God's deeds and wonders that He performed for us from the day of the Exodus from Egypt until today. As it is written: "You shall make known to your children and to your children's children."[3]

All-Merciful One! Grant us the light of true vision by which we can gaze and behold the truth always, by which we can gaze and behold God's wonders always, in truth! Open my eyes and the eyes of all Israel, and we will behold the wonders of Your Torah which You revealed through Your true tzaddikim. You alone know the wondrousness of the Torah they revealed to the world.

Through the light of this vision, may all the requests and supplications that we have prayed ascend to the Heavenly Holy Temple. Awaken the Redemption which depends on the heart, as it is written: "For a day of retribution is in My Heart, and the year of My Redemption has come."[4]

Nullify from our midst the leaven and chametz of the "evil inclination of the human heart that remains within us from our youth."[5] This is the leaven and chametz of the heart that entice a person to entertain doubts about the Torah sages of the generation, saying, "This one is appealing, and that one is unappealing."[6] This causes our hearts to be divided, and the "seventy-two tzaddikim of the generation"[7] to be concealed from us, so that we do not clearly recognize one of them.

Have mercy on us for Your sake and remove, destroy and nullify the leaven and chametz within our hearts until we become capable of believing in all the tzaddikim, and no longer entertain any doubts whatsoever about them, or make any distinctions between them at all. Rather, may they all be extremely beautiful, beloved and precious in our eyes.

As a result, may we merit that our hearts be inflamed with enthusiasm in our study of the Torah, with flames of love; and the "many waters" of extraneous loves and fears "will not be able to extinguish the love, nor will rivers drown it."[8]

(LT II, 42)

Notes

1. Paraphrase of Exodus 4:11.
2. Psalms 78:6.
3. Deuteronomy 4:9.
4. Isaiah 63:4.
5. Paraphrase of Genesis 8:21.

6   Cf. *Eruvin* 64a. See *Likutey Moharan* I, 5:4; ibid., 56:10.
7   See *Sukkah* 45b; *Sanhedrin* 97b. According to the *Zohar*, there are thirty-six hidden tzaddikim in the Land of Israel and thirty-six in the Diaspora; see *Tikkuney Zohar, Tikkun* 21, 50a.
8   Song of Songs 8:7.

72

Expanded Consciousness

Matzah is a spiritual food that expands the mind and gives the Jew a taste of the most sublime concepts.

Master of the Universe! Help me to attain holy memory – to remember the words of Your Torah constantly and not let them slip from my memory, in fulfillment of the verse: "They shall not cease from your mouth, nor from the mouth of your children, nor from the mouth of your children's children, says God, from now until the end of time."[1]

Protect me from violating the prohibition of possessing even the smallest amount of chametz throughout the days of Pesach. Through this, may I be saved from falling into states of constricted consciousness that lead to all harsh judgments and all sufferings, God forbid. May I be worthy of seeing beyond the illusion of nature completely and eliciting the full manifestation of Divine Providence, which comes from expanded consciousness.

Grant me the privilege of eating matzah on the days of Pesach and, by so doing, attaining the perception of Divine Providence – to truly believe that the natural order is an illusion, and that everything takes place through Your Providence alone; to negate all perplexities and heretical ideas that befall humankind because of Your hidden ways; and to believe that all that transpires is for the good. We can accomplish all this by eating matzah in a state of holiness. Through the merit of eating matzah, may we be granted revelations of Godliness, to see and to know that everything reflects Your Providence.

(Tefilot HaBoker, Tefilah 7)

Notes

1   Isaiah 59:21; cf. Joshua 1:8 as cited in *Bava Metzia* 85a. The latter is the subject of *Likutey Moharan* I, 110.

Sefirat HaOmer
Counting the Omer

73

Entering the Gates of Holiness

Day by day, the mitzvah of counting the Omer brings us closer to God, opening all the gates of holiness and purity.

Master of the Universe! "Remember Your mercies, O God, and Your kindnesses, for they are everlasting!"[1] Remember Your wondrous and awesome acts of benevolence which You performed by taking us out of Egypt "with great strength and a mighty Hand."[2] You revealed to us the truth of faith in Your Divinity with a profound, wondrous and ecstatic illumination, and performed awesome miracles in order to reveal Your Godliness, Your Oneness and "Your dominion, which extends over all."[3]

Then You drew us near to You to be a holy nation, extricated us from the Forty-Nine Gates of Impurity, and ushered us into the Forty-Nine Gates of Holiness. These are the Forty-Nine Gates of Repentance rooted in the forty-nine letters of the names of the Twelve Tribes.

In Your great compassion, You commanded us to count the forty-nine days of the Omer that correspond to these Forty-Nine Gates and forty-nine letters, thus to cleanse our souls; and through the mitzvah of counting the Omer, to be spiritually transformed – to leave the Forty-Nine Gates of Impurity and enter the Forty-Nine Gates of Holiness.

Master of the Universe! All-Merciful One! Grant us the privilege of fulfilling the mitzvah of counting the Omer in its proper time, with great holiness and awesome and wondrous fervor. With the holiness of this mitzvah, may we be aroused to return to You sincerely and leave behind all forms of impurity, and purge ourselves of all corruption that may still cling to us due to our evil deeds.

Master of the Universe! Master of the Universe! Save us with all deliverances! You know the vast power of each and every mitzvah – how any mitzvah can extricate us from the places to which we have fallen because of our many transgressions, and help us to draw close to You. This especially applies to the mitzvah of counting the Omer, which is a preparation to receiving the Torah on Shavuot. By counting the Omer, we re-enact the beginning of Israel's drawing close to their Heavenly Father, for You gave us this sacred mitzvah to enable us to leave the Forty-Nine Gates of Impurity and enter the Forty-Nine Gates of Holiness.

Confer merit upon me in the very place I now find myself, that I may fulfill this mitzvah to the ultimate degree possible for a person of my spiritual level. Pour forth Your mercy on me, and help me and save me through this. Speedily bring me from impurity to purity, from the profane to the sacred, from grief to joy, from servitude to freedom, from darkness to brilliant light – until on the holy festival of Shavuot, on the fiftieth day, You return to us and open for us the Fiftieth Gate. From there, You will express the fullness of Your abundant mercy and lovingkindness. Then we will merit to rectify everything spiritually, and return to You in truth.

(LT II, 36)

Notes

1 Psalms 25:6.
2 Paraphrase of Nehemiah 1:10.
3 Paraphrase of Psalms 103:19.

74

Keys to the Royal Palace

Reb Noson continues his theme of opening the Forty-Nine Gates of Repentance as he expresses thanks for the Book of Psalms, which can awaken the Ten Types of Melody and heal Israel's collective soul.

"You formed Your world from olden times"[1] for the sake of Israel, Your chosen nation. In Your great mercy, You conferred merit upon us and gave us Your holy Torah through Moses, Your prophet and trusted servant, "to sustain us in life until this day,"[2] so that through the Torah we might attain the "day that is entirely good and entirely enduring."[3]

In Your vast beneficence, You showed us additional kindnesses and wondrous favors through the tzaddikim of all generations, who made "handles" for the Torah, safeguards upon safeguards.[4] "How many sublime favors the Omnipresent One performed for us,"[5] until we were deemed worthy of such profuse kindnesses and expressions of compassion, "faithful kindnesses of David,"[6] in that You graced us with kindness and favor beyond what You had shown us already, in order to enliven our souls. You sent us a deliverer and master, "anointed one of the God of Jacob, sweet singer of Israel"[7] – King David, "who lives and endures,"[8] who composed the holy and awesome Book of Psalms, five books corresponding to the Five Books of the Torah.

"How great is Your goodness"[9] that You performed for us! "How can I repay God for all the bounty that He has conferred upon us?"[10] In Your abundant mercy,

You revealed to us that by reciting psalms, we may attain teshuvah. For You desire kindness, and favor the repentance of the wicked, and do not wish for their demise.[11] Therefore You "preceded our sickness with its cure"[12] and graced us with this holy Book of Psalms, which can open for us all the Gates of Mercy and all the Gates of Repentance. These are the Fifty Gates of Repentance which correspond to the Fifty Gates of Understanding.[13]

Master of the Universe! Merciful Father! Grant me the privilege of reciting psalms all my days! Help me and all the members of my family, together with all Israel, Your people, to recite many psalms each day, fervently and wholeheartedly. Let me incline my heart well, so that my ears hear the words expressed by my mouth. Through all of life's ups and downs, may I find myself in the verses of the psalms, which incorporate all souls and all spiritual levels, from the loftiest heights to the lowest depths – so that all fallen souls, even the most utterly estranged, can find themselves in the Book of Psalms.

By reciting psalms, everyone can awaken his heart to return to God completely and arrive at the Gate of Repentance that is designated for him, corresponding to his letter among the forty-nine letters of the names of the Twelve Tribes. For these letters correspond to the Forty-Nine Gates of Repentance through which we must pass in order to return to God – until God returns to us, so to speak, in complete teshuvah, confers upon us the highest degree of Divine mercy, and helps us to draw close to Him always, no matter where we have fallen. Thus we will return in complete teshuvah by engaging in one level of repentance after the other, continually.[14]

Master of the Universe, help me to recite numerous psalms regularly, every day, with intense concentration, wondrous fervor and sincere intentions, until I come to feel the pain of my sins, and repent completely.

Let me also rejoice greatly by reciting psalms, and awaken all Ten Types of Melody; for these Ten Types of Melody accomplish the healing of the Queen's Daughter, who represents the collective soul of Israel.[15] "Let us play my melodies all the days of our lives in the House of God"[16] with a voice of song and thanksgiving. "For God is good, His kindness endures forever!"[17]

All-Merciful One, take me out of the Egyptian exile! Release me from all states of exile of body and soul, all of which are called "Egyptian exile." Let me attain purity and spiritual cleansing, and discover all Forty-Nine Gates of Repentance by reciting the holy psalms, which incorporate all forty-nine letters of the names of the Children of Israel who descended to Egypt. In this way, You will extricate me from the Forty-Nine Gates of Impurity and allow me to enter the Forty-Nine Gates of Holiness.

Let my throat not become hoarse from calling out to You again and again. Bring me into wide-open spaces and raise me up from the paradigm of Egypt – which is called the "narrowness of the throat," the paradigm of spiritual constriction – until I open my mouth and You fill it with all true and eternal good. Help me to return to You in complete teshuvah with all my "heart and soul and wealth."[18]

"Return us, O God of our deliverance, and annul Your anger with us."[19] "Bring us back to You, O God, and we will return; renew our days as of old!"[20]

(LT II, 36)

Notes

1. Paraphrase of liturgy, Shabbat Rosh Chodesh *Shemoneh Esrei*.
2. Paraphrase of Deuteronomy 6:24.
3. Liturgy, Yom Tov *Birkat HaMazon* (Grace After Meals), end; also see the explanation of Rabbi Yisrael Chaim Friedman, *Likutey Maharich*, Vol. I, *Birkat HaMazon*, s.v. *"HaRachaman Hu yanchileinu le'yom shekulo tov"* (Chatzor, 1991 ed., p. 248).
4. *Tamid* 26a.
5. Paraphrase of Pesach Haggadah.
6. Paraphrase of Isaiah 55:3. In Kabbalistic works, this alludes to the sefirot of Netzach and Hod, which transmit Divine influence and blessing to Malkhut; e.g. Rabbi Chaim Vital, *Sha'ar HaKavanot, Kavanot HaAmidah, Drush* 3.
7. II Samuel 23:1.
8. Liturgy, *Kiddush Levanah*, based on *Rosh HaShanah* 25a.
9. Paraphrase of Psalms 31:20.
10. Paraphrase of Psalms 116:12.
11. Liturgy, Yom Kippur *Ne'ilah*.
12. *Megillah* 13a.
13. *Rosh HaShanah* 21b states that there are Fifty Gates of Understanding, all but one of which were attained by Moses; also see *Zohar* II, 115a, II, 216a; et al. The Baal Shem Tov explains that Moses could not attain the Fiftieth Gate during his mortal existence because it is the first gate of the next "set" on the transcendental plane; see *Toldot Yaakov Yosef, Devarim* (176a); also *Sefer Baal Shem Tov, Mishpatim* 23. Chassidic master Rabbi Aharon HaKohen of Zhelikhov mentions this concept in connection with meditative prayer; see *Ohr HaGanuz LeTzaddikim, Mattot*, translated in my anthology of early Chassidic teachings, *The Path of the Baal Shem Tov* (Jason Aronson, 1997), pp. 26-27.
14. See *Likutey Moharan* I, 6, which explains that a person must repent continually for his lack of absolute sincerity on previous occasions of repentance. Even a tzaddik who has completely purged his heart of the evil inclination must engage in teshuvah constantly on account of his previous conception of God. Since God is Infinite and "His greatness is beyond investigation"

(Psalms 145:3), any conception one has of God is inevitably limited and faulty. Therefore the tzaddik must repent for this, too.

15 In Rebbe Nachman's *Tale of the Seven Beggars* (*Rabbi Nachman's Stories* #13), on the sixth day of the wedding celebration, the Beggar With No Hands arrives to give the bride and groom his spiritual gift: the unique power of his hands, which, despite their seeming incapacity, possess the highest powers of charity, healing, music-making and, implicitly, prophecy. His "approbation" for his claim to possess these powers comes from the Water Castle, the central symbol of yet another story within a story. The Beggar With No Hands relates how an evil king captured a princess; she escaped and found refuge in the Water Castle. The evil king's soldiers pursued her and struck her with ten poisoned arrows, causing her to collapse in the innermost precincts of the Water Castle. "But I heal her with my ten fingers," declares the Beggar With No Hands. In Rebbe Nachman's allegory, the princess represents Knesset Yisrael (the collective soul of the Jewish people) as well as each individual soul in its quest for tikkun; the evil king is the evil inclination; the Water Castle is the Torah; and the Beggar represents the *tzaddik emet* (true tzaddik); see Rabbi Nachman of Tcherin, *Rimzey HaMa'asiyot*, ad loc.

16 Isaiah 38:20.
17 Psalms 100:5.
18 Paraphrase of Rashi on Deuteronomy 6:5.
19 Psalms 85:5.
20 Lamentations 5:21.

75

Connecting Sefirat HaOmer to Purim

The Torah is a unified system in which every mitzvah interrelates with every other. Here Reb Noson connects the mitzvah of counting the Omer with the mitzvot of Purim.

Grant me the privilege of fulfilling the mitzvah of counting the Omer in holiness and purity, wholeheartedly and with great joy, with all its details, fine points and intentions, as well as the complete structure of 613 mitzvot that depend on it.[1] In this way, may I subjugate, destroy, uproot and nullify the kelipah of Haman-Amalek[2] from the world. Mercifully help us to greet the days of Purim with great joy; and may we draw forth the holiness of the light of Purim, the holiness of Mordekhai and Esther, upon ourselves, our children, and Your entire people, the House of Israel.

Let us fulfill all the mitzvot that are related to Purim in holiness and purity, joyously and wholeheartedly. Instill joy in our hearts until it spreads to our hands and feet, so that we clap and dance in holiness, with the greatest ecstasy, for Your Name's sake!

In Your mercy, enable us to accept upon ourselves anew the fulfillment of the words of Your Torah with love. May we study, teach, observe, perform and uphold Your Torah. Enlighten our eyes with its wisdom. May we merit to learn, understand and truly comprehend its revealed and hidden dimensions. Grant us the privilege of grasping Divine mysteries constantly, "so that we do not come before You without merit."[3]

(LT I, 10)

Notes

1 See p. 89, note 2.
2 "Haman-Amalek" refers to a kelipah (unholy force) rather than two of the historical enemies of the Jewish people. This kelipah stands in opposition to faith, and will be destroyed at the End of Days.
3 Cf. *Zohar* III, 287b.

Lag BaOmer
33rd Day of the Omer

76

In the Merit of Rabbi Shimon bar Yochai

In this prayer based on Rebbe Nachman's teaching about Rabbi Shimon bar Yochai (Likutey Moharan I, beginning), Reb Noson invokes Rabbi Shimon and the other tzaddikim who "rest in the dust" to intercede on behalf of the Jewish people. May they help us to overcome all our obstacles and fulfill our spiritual mission as bearers of God's Torah.

Rabbi Shimon bar Yochai, "holy awakened being descended from Heaven,"[1] holy lamp, supernal lamp, mighty lamp, precious lamp! You promised the Jewish people that through you, the Torah would never be forgotten by Israel, when you declared: "With this book, the *Zohar*, you will go forth from exile!"[2] Even in the "double concealment"[3] of holiness that prevails during these times known as the "footsteps of the Mashiach," you promised us that the Torah would not be forgotten by our descendants, as it is written: "And I shall surely hide My Face on that day because of all the evil that [Israel] did. ... Then this song shall speak up before it as a witness, for it shall not be forgotten from the mouth of its descendants."[4]

The days have finally arrived that we never wished to see![5] Our exile has gone on so long, and our servitude has persisted. Every day we wander in poverty and our power has fallen greatly – "for the enemy's power increases, and none is saved or assisted."[6] We remain like fatherless orphans, and there is none to take up our cause.

Yet in the adversity of these last days of our bitter exile, the light of Mashiach has already begun to glimmer, starting from the days of the ARI, blessed be the memory of the tzaddik. Your nation, the House of Israel, now yearns and longs for God, and we all desire to revere Your Name with the most intense yearning, the likes of which never existed before,[7] "even if I were constantly awake, and always with You."[8]

I have arrived at the end of all generations, and still I am with You! We still cling to You and yearn to serve You, until our souls are about to leave us!

At the same time, our distance from You today is immeasurable. "We are drowning in the watery abyss without a foothold. We have entered the deep water, and the rushing current sweeps us away!"[9] Your people, Israel, have rebelled so greatly that it is impossible to describe the incitement of the Evil One, who has attacked us so severely and caused us to fall so low.

Who am I, in my spiritual poverty, to recount the troubles of Israel? O God, You alone know the full extent of Israel's plight in these times, at the End of Days. Nevertheless, I have come to speak and bewail the state of my soul – how far I am from God and how extensive are my spiritual damage, my many transgressions and my enormous sins. "Over these I weep; my eyes, my eyes flow with tears!"[10]

I do not know any way to regain the power of holiness and attain perfect repentance. I do not know of any path to begin to forsake my evil ways and my despicable thoughts, or how to remedy such spiritual disasters as these. O my soul, I don't know where to go. Where can I take my profound disgrace? Where can I flee? Where can I hide because of my embarrassment and shame? I "call to the mountains, 'Cover me!' and to the hills, 'Fall on me!'"[11] Woe for what has happened to me! Woe for what has happened to me!

"Therefore I said, 'Leave me alone, I will weep bitter tears!'"[12] "Perhaps He will have pity! Perhaps He will have mercy!"[13] "Nothing prevents God from saving"[14] even me, at this very time – for there is great relief and salvation before Him, as it is written: "You can do anything, and nothing can hinder Your objective."[15]

My teacher, my teacher, my teacher! "My father, my father! Chariot of Israel and its rider!"[16] Light of the lamp of Torah! Awaken! Why do you sleep? How is it possible to endure the sufferings of Israel? Arise and awaken, together with all the true tzaddikim, to gaze upon and behold the affliction of our souls! "Awaken and sing, all who rest in the dust!"[17] Arise, sleepers of Makhpelah,[18] to our support! Righteous pillars of the world, come to our assistance at this hour of crisis! Have compassion and mercy on the entire flock of the Children of Israel, myself among them – although I am sinful, spiritually damaged and full of transgressions from head to foot.

You know all the travail we have encountered from the day we went into exile until now, everything that each of us has endured. In particular, You know what I have gone through from the day the three levels of my soul and my body were "emanated, created, formed and made"[19]; what I have endured in each successive incarnation – especially what I have endured in my present body; everything I have ever experienced until today, what I remember, and what I have forgotten.

It would take "all the lambs of Nevayot"[20] to create enough parchment to describe a fraction of the damage I have caused in one day, given the spiritual repercussions

LAG BAOMER

of my actions according to the root of my soul – and all the more so, all the damage I have caused in the course of all my days, from the first to the last. Who could describe this, who could measure this? What can I say? What can I answer? What can I declare? How can I exonerate myself?

Master of the Universe! Inspire the heart of this holy awesome tzaddik, Rabbi Shimon bar Yochai [if one is privileged to stand at his gravesite, add: "who rests here"], as well as the hearts of all true tzaddikim, not to hide their faces from me, but to stand up for me as eloquent defenders, to review my merits, and to search until they find good points in me. Thus will they intercede on my behalf, begging You in Your mercy to draw me close to You and grant me "a new heart and a new spirit."[21] Then I will be able to arouse myself truly to return to You, from now on, sincerely and wholeheartedly. "Heavens, pray for us!"[22] May all merciful and compassionate ones have mercy on me! May all those who rest in the dust intercede on behalf of one who is "drowning in the deep with no foothold"[23] like me!

Rabbi Shimon bar Yochai! Let us remember and take to heart that in these generations we merited to hear about your wondrous and awesome greatness – how the Torah hints that through you, the Torah shall not be forgotten. Because the final letters of the verse you cited as a proof: *"KI lO tishakhaCh mipI zarO* – For it shall not be forgotten from the mouths of your children"[24] spell YOChAI, your father's holy name. And a different verse hints at your own holy name: *"Ir Vekadish Min Shemaya Nachit* – A holy awakening being descended from Heaven,"[25] the initial letters of which spell ShIMON.

You alone know the hidden meaning of these mysteries. You alone know the greatness of the assurance you gave to the Jewish people that through you, the Torah would not be forgotten from Israel, and how Moses our teacher prophesied concerning this in the holy Torah long before!

Therefore I have come to recall this. Please, my holy masters! Have pity on me and do not consider all the evil I have done from time immemorial until today, in thought, speech and action, "for I rebelled against the words of God and despised the advice of the Supreme One."[26] Do not gaze upon my evil deeds and do not treat me as I deserve, according to my sins. Let me not be a thorn in your eyes, after all the times you tried to arouse me with thousands and myriads of hints and arousals, and with so many kinds of good advice to draw nearer to God every day and every moment. Despite all your efforts, in my stubbornness I continued to ruin my life and did not incline my ears or my heart to your advice.

Have compassion on me and do not pay attention to any of this. Do not allow your anger to burn against me, God forbid. Instead, devise new strategies to put an end to my banishment from God and from you, from now on. For there is no impediment to God's deliverance even now. I have no strength but with my mouth alone – and this too comes from God, Who did not withhold His kindness and His truth from me, but gave strength to a weary person like me, that I may now speak these few words.

Upon this I have staked my confidence: that the tzaddikim will have mercy on me and take action, so that I may return to God in truth. May I go to the Land of

Israel speedily and in peace, and say all this and more at your holy resting places!

Tzaddikim! Holy sages! God in His goodness will surely hear your prayers! For your sake He will help, protect and save me, together with the entire Jewish people. He will bring me back speedily in perfect teshuvah to Him, pick me up and not let me go. He will not despise or reject me in any way, until at last I return to Him in truth, and conduct myself according to His beneficent will forever. In this lifetime, may I fix all the damage I have done, in the power and merit of the true tzaddikim upon whom I rely exclusively, as I have composed these words of mine before them and before the All-Merciful One, Knower of Secrets!

"God will finish everything for me. O God, Your kindness endures forever; do not forsake the work of Your Hand!"[27] "Take my soul out of prison, so that I may praise Your Name; the tzaddikim will crown You because of me, when You have dealt kindly with me!"[28]

(LT II, 47)

Notes

1 Daniel 4:10.
2 *Zohar* III, 124b. Rebbe Nachman discusses this pronouncement in the lesson, "*Lekhu Chazu Nifla'ot HaShem* – Come, Behold the Wonders of God," printed immediately before the first discourse in *Likutey Moharan*.
3 This echoes the verse, "For I will surely hide (*haster astir*, a double expression of concealment) My Face on that day" (Deuteronomy 31:18). Not only is God's light hidden, but also the very fact of its hiddenness is hidden, as Rebbe Nachman explains in *Likutey Moharan* I, 56:3, s.v. *ki yesh shnei hastarot*.

4 Deuteronomy 31:18, 21.
5 Cf. *Sanhedrin* 98b: "Let him [the Mashiach] come, but let me not see it!"
6 Deuteronomy 32:36, according to Rashi.
7 Cf. Amos 8:11. See also *Sichot HaRan* 259, 260; *Chayey Moharan* 554; et passim, on the importance of longing and thirsting for God.
8 Psalms 139:18.
9 Paraphrase of Psalms 69:3.
10 Lamentations 1:16.
11 Paraphrase of Hosea 10:8.
12 Isaiah 22:4.
13 Liturgy, *Selichot*.
14 I Samuel 14:6.
15 Job 42:2.
16 II Kings 2:12. Reb Noson echoes the words which Elisha the Prophet cried out when he witnessed the Heavenly ascent of his master, Elijah the Prophet, on a fiery chariot drawn by horses of fire.
17 Isaiah 26:19.
18 An allusion to the patriarchs and matriarchs (with the exception of Rachel) who are buried in the Cave of Makhpelah in Chevron.
19 An allusion to the Four Worlds of *Atzilut* (Emanation), *Beri'ah* (Creation), *Yetzirah* (Formation) and *Asiyah* (Action).
20 Paraphrase of Isaiah 60:7.
21 Paraphrase of Ezekiel 36:26.
22 Liturgy, *Selichot*.
23 Op cit.
24 Deuteronomy 31:21.
25 Daniel 4:10.
26 Paraphrase of Psalms 107:11.
27 Psalms 138:8.
28 Psalms 142:8, according to Rashi.

Shavuot
The Festival of Weeks

77

The Fiftieth Gate

Shavuot, which occurs on the fiftieth day after the beginning of the counting of the Omer, is called a "mikveh," as it represents the Fiftieth Gate, the ultimate level of holiness. As we immerse in the mikveh in honor of this holy day, we pray that God will cleanse us of all impurities and enable us to draw close to Him.

Help us and deliver us, so that we may purify and sanctify ourselves at all times by immersing in the mikveh. May we cleanse ourselves of all forms of impurity – all sins, transgressions and iniquities that we have committed before You, from our youth until today – and elicit great holiness through the mikveh.

Confer upon us higher consciousness and abundant mercy in the merit of immersing in the mikveh; and grant us the power to mitigate all harsh judgments against us, our offspring and the entire House of Israel through our immersion. Remove all afflictions, cancel all evil decrees and save us constantly through the holy and awesome mikveh, in fulfillment of the verse: "O Hope (*Mikveh*) of Israel, its Redeemer in a time of distress."[1]

Grant us the privilege to draw upon ourselves the holiness of the mikveh of Shavuot, the day that commemorates the Giving of Your Torah – when Israel came close to You and were deemed worthy to receive the holy Torah through immersing in the mikveh.[2] On Shavuot, may we all be granted the merit of being cleansed in the Supernal Mikveh – the mikveh of the Fiftieth Gate of Holiness, which is great and eternal mercy, sublime lovingkindness and highly exalted consciousness.

SHAVUOT

Enable us to transmit the holiness of this mikveh of Shavuot to the entire year. May we purify and sanctify ourselves constantly, exit all Fifty Gates of Impurity, and enter the Fifty Gates of Holiness.

As it is written: "I will sprinkle upon you pure water, that you may be cleansed; and from your contamination and from all your idols, I will purify you!"[3]

(LT I, 56)

Notes

1. Jeremiah 14:8. The word *mikveh* literally means "expectation" or "hope"; alternately, it refers to the pool of water into which a person immerses to obtain ritual purification.
2. *Yevamot* 46b, citing Exodus 19:10.
3. Ezekiel 36:25.

78

Perfecting God's Kingship

By entering the holiness of Shavuot and garbing ourselves in the holy teachings of the true tzaddikim, we effect great changes in the supernal worlds and recognize God's Sovereignty over our own world.

Master of the Universe! Grant me the privilege of going to a kosher mikveh every day and immersing before prayer. By immersing in the mikveh, may I draw upon myself higher consciousness and overflowing kindness from Above, which has its source in the mikveh of Shavuot. Thus may the holy attribute of Malkhut attain true perfection – through the mikveh of Shavuot, which is supernal kindness and abundant mercy.

We draw all this upon ourselves by virtue of the Torah of the true tzaddikim. Through their holy teachings, we imbue ourselves with supernal kindness and knowledge, until we will perceive that You are present within all concealments. In this way, we will leave all places of concealment and truly recognize that You reign supreme over the entire world. Your Kingship extends over all, as it is written: "God is King forever and ever; the nations have perished from His Land."[1]

May we be privileged to make known Your faith and Your Sovereignty from generation to generation – that "Your kingdom extends over all worlds, and Your dominion from generation to generation"[2] – and bring others back in perfect teshuvah. "For God is good, His kindness is everlasting, and His faithfulness is from generation to generation."[3] "God will rule forever."[4] Amen and amen!

(Tefilot HaBoker)

Notes

1. Psalms 10:16. The Canaanite nations that dwelled in the Holy Land before the Jewish people entered it represent the paradigm of idolatry and the concealment of God's Kingship.
2. Psalms 145:13.
3. Psalms 100:5.
4. Psalms 146:10.

Bein HaMetzarim

The Three Weeks of Mourning Over Jerusalem

79

Turning "Mourning" into "Morning"

We long for the coming of the Mashiach, anticipating the day when the world will achieve its ultimate tikkun. How wonderful it will be to see this world of conflict, exploitation and spiritual ignorance transformed into a realm of peace, lovingkindness and Divine wisdom!

O God and God of our fathers, have mercy on us and send our righteous Mashiach right away, and perfect this world and all worlds – from the highest to the lowest – all of which depend on this world of action. Have pity on him and on us, and bring him speedily, in peace. For the Mashiach will rectify everything with a most wondrous and awesome tikkun. He will enlighten us with true sublime knowledge and open our eyes and hearts to Your Torah. Through him we will come to understand the words of the Torah lucidly, according to their true meaning. No doubt or question about any law or practice among the laws and practices of the Torah will remain confusing to us, but everything will be "as clear as a white cloth."[1]

Even all the questions and doubts which perplexed the great tzaddikim of former times – concerning which our sages said, "*Teyku*"[2] – will be straightened out, clarified and made comprehensible to us. The Mashiach will rectify the paradigm of *teyku* that includes all doubts in the world – both those doubts of an encompassing nature that perplexed the eminent sages of Israel regarding the laws and practices of the Torah, and those doubts and inner conflicts that beset each person, from the greatest to the smallest.

So many of Your children long and yearn to return to You, yet the paths of teshuvah and the paths of Torah are hidden from them because their hearts are torn by all sorts of doubts and conflicting ideas. This especially applies to me today. You know how much I have suffered because of my doubts and uncertainties about almost everything! Even now, my heart is torn by confusion and conflict about so many matters. My mind is so agitated that it seems almost unbearable.

Master of the Universe, Lord, God of truth, "great in counsel, and great in deed!"³ Have mercy on the Jewish people and on me, and send us a wondrous illumination from the World of Tikkun, an illumination brought about by our righteous Mashiach. Then the problem of *teyku* will be solved at last – all questions will be resolved, all doubts and the slightest "doubts of doubts" clarified, and we will attain perfect advice in truth, constantly and in all circumstances.

In Your mercy, show us the true way to mourn and lament over the destruction of the Holy Temple, particularly every night at the actual moment of chatzot, as well as during the Three Weeks; and especially on Tisha B'Av, help us to recite the Book of Lamentations and the *kinot* with a truly broken heart. "Let us pour out our hearts like water before God's Face."⁴ "Let us put our faces to the dust; perhaps there is yet hope!"⁵

It has been so many centuries since our city, Jerusalem, was razed, the site of our Holy Temple left desolate, and God's glory removed from the House of our life. Every day's troubles seem worse than those of the day before⁶ – especially now, when exceptionally harsh decrees have been imposed on the Jewish people that are beyond our endurance. Our lives hang by a thread due to the dread in our hearts when we hear of still more harsh decrees that our oppressors wish to impose on us, God forbid. May the Merciful One spare us! Woe unto us for what has befallen us!

God full of mercy! Help us to take to heart the sufferings of Israel, as well as our own spiritual plight, until we break our hearts before You in truth, and "pour out our hearts like water before the Face of the Lord, God of Hosts," over our iniquities, our many sins and our stiff-necked refusal to change, which have prolonged our exile and caused all our troubles.

"Let us lift up our hearts in our hands unto God in Heaven!"[7] Let us emulate our holy ancestors, and cry and scream and wail bitterly! Let us "wander through the market stalls and the streets"[8] and pray, beseech, cry out and entreat, until God "looks down from Heaven and sees"[9] – until He awakens His compassion toward us and consoles us speedily, and delivers us from all affliction and suffering, collectively and individually.

Shine upon us, even now, a wondrous illumination from our righteous Mashiach. Sweeten all harsh judgments and remove all suffering, affliction and evil decrees from us and from all Israel. Enlighten us with the light of truth at all times, perfect us constantly with new and wondrous tikkunim, and clarify and make comprehensible to us all doubts, questions and conflicting views. May we always attain perfect advice, in truth, so that we may return to You speedily, sincerely and wholeheartedly, and engage in Torah study, prayer, mitzvot and good deeds all the days of our lives.

Protect us and save us constantly from all sins, transgressions and evil deeds, and may we never veer from performing Your will, "neither to the right or the left."[10] Arouse Your compassion on behalf of Your children, speedily bring us our righteous Mashiach, and redeem us with the Final Redemption, the Eternal Redemption. Then You will transform the aspect of *teyku* to tikkun, to the ultimate degree of perfection. The letter *nun* from *kinot* will be added to the word *teyku* to form the word *tikkun*. Thus all *kinot* will be removed from the world and transformed into tikkun.

Merciful One, Master of Deliverance, Master of Consolation! Console us after all our sufferings and assist us in all our strivings. Spread over us Your tent of peace, send us good advice, and save us quickly for the sake of Your Name. Show us the absolute truth. Save us from doubts and conflicts that deter and confuse our attempts to serve You. Send us the right advice at all times so that we may return to You in truth, and adhere to Your benevolent will, now and forever. Amen!

(LT I, 142)

Notes

1. Cf. Rashi on Deuteronomy 22:17.
2. *TeYKU* is the acronym for "*Tishbi Yetaretz Kushiyot U'ba'ayot* – The Tishbite (i.e., Elijah the Prophet) will answer difficulties and questions," a formula used by the Talmudic sages as a last resort when they confronted irresolvable contradictions. The reference to Elijah portends the coming of Mashiach, who will resolve all contradictions and enable the Jewish people to fulfill the Torah in its entirety.
3. Jeremiah 32:19.

4 Paraphrase of Lamentations 2:19.
5 Paraphrase of Lamentations 3:29.
6 Reb Noson alludes to one of the "birth pangs of the Mashiach," recounted in the *beraita* of Rabbi Pinchas ben Ya'ir, appended to *Sotah* 9:15.
7 Lamentations 3:41.
8 Paraphrase of Song of Songs 3:2.
9 Paraphrase of Isaiah 63:15; et al.
10 Paraphrase of Deuteronomy 17:11. In Kabbalistic terminology, the "right" represents the attribute of Chesed (Kindness), while the "left" represents the attribute of Gevurah (Judgment).

80

Light Conquers Fire

Based on the lesson of Likutey Moharan II, 67, Reb Noson composed this heartfelt lament over the destruction of the Holy Temple and the death of the tzaddikim, in particular Rebbe Nachman. Giving vent to all his feelings of devastation after his teacher's passing, Reb Noson underscores the nature and magnitude of his loss and how it could be remedied. Many Breslover Chassidim recite this prayer on Tisha B'Av in addition to the traditional laments.

"A voice is heard on high, a lament, bitter weeping. Rachel cries for her children. She refuses to be consoled over her children, for they are gone."[1]

"For these I weep. My eye, my eye pours forth tears, for my comforter, the restorer of my soul, is far from me. My children are devastated, because the enemy has prevailed."[2]

Master of the Universe! Master of the Universe! Teach us how to compose bitter eulogies over the vastness of our tragedy, which we have suffered because of our straying hearts. We have lost the delight of our eyes, our majesty, our crowns, our splendor, our radiance, our beauty, our life and length of days – the source of our spirits and souls! Are these not our masters, our teachers and our sages? They were our light, our greatness, our holiness, our hope, our destiny, our consolation, our joy, our Torah and our prayer. To eternal rest their souls departed without warning, leaving us to grieve and mourn.

Woe for what has happened to us! What can we say? What words can we speak? Who can compose bitter laments for us, so that we may mourn and cry over these tragedies that affect every member of the Jewish people and all the worlds, from the highest to the lowest? Woe unto us!

Master of the Universe! It is known and revealed before You that no human being is capable of composing befitting eulogies over the demise of tzaddikim such as these, who passed away in our generations due to our sins. However, this I must surely mourn, because it is a loss that affects me and the entire Jewish people.

There is no loss for the holy tzaddikim who have ascended to far loftier planes, for they are greatly esteemed in the supernal worlds where they continue to perform their service on high. Fortunate are they – fortunate is their lot!

But as for us, this orphaned generation, this spiritually impoverished generation, our plight is pathetic. Upon us, upon us, all sickness has fallen! "Woe unto us, for we have been vanquished!"[3] O God, we are bowed down in anguish, our arms are weak, our knees totter, our hearts have melted and turned to water on this day when the sun sets at noon! "We are stricken with confusion, tremors have seized us, pangs have overcome us like the travail of a woman in childbirth."[4]

Heavenly Father, Merciful Father, Lord, God of truth! Where shall we go? Where shall we turn for help? Who will assist us? Who will take up our cause? "Where has our Beloved gone, where has our Beloved gone? Let us seek Him with You!"[5] All day long our words are embittered; our arms weigh heavily upon us, due to our groaning.

Would that our heads flowed with water and our eyes gave forth streams of tears so that we could weep day and night over the vastness of our tragedy! "Over this our hearts were sick, over these our eyes were dimmed!"[6]

Master of the Universe! Truly Merciful Father! You know that all our vitality depends on the tzaddikim, our holy rabbis of blessed memory. We need to speak with them, receive holy words from them, and see them all the time. Now what will happen? What can we do, people of low stature like ourselves, who are like "hyssop that grows out of the wall"[7]? What can we do? What can we accomplish?

Master of the Universe, Master of the Universe! You alone know the anguish of my soul within me, how my soul is embittered over this. But due to my many sins, I am unable to express my feelings in words before You, O Merciful One.

Master of the Universe, what is past is past. Beginning now, teach me how to cry and supplicate and plead before You, so that even now I may draw forth their holiness by means of the after-impression of holiness that remains in this world through their holy books and precious disciples. They are present in the world to an even greater degree after their passing, as is written in the holy *Zohar* and other sacred works.[8] For the soul achieves completeness primarily when it ascends above to the supernal worlds, yet at the same time remains below to arouse, awaken and enliven all souls, even those sunken in the lowest depths of hell, so that they never succumb to despair in any way.[9]

Master of the Universe, have compassion for the sake of the tears of our mother Rachel, who personifies the

Shekhinah and Knesset Yisrael (the collective soul of the Jewish people). She cries inconsolably over our suffering and spiritual anguish, as it is written: "Rachel cries over her children"[10] – those who have been banished from their Father's table and sent away from their Land. "She weeps bitterly in the night, and her tear lies upon her cheek; from all her lovers, she has no comforter"[11] – because all her friends – the tzaddikim of every generation – have passed away, due to our many sins. We remain forlorn "like a mast atop a mountain, and a banner on a lonely hill."[12] "We have become like orphans without a father, our mothers are like widows,"[13] and there is no one to console us.

Master of the Universe! Who will show us pity? Who will show us compassion? Who will deplore our plight? Who will turn aside to inquire after our welfare? Who will shore up a rampart or stand in the breach? Who will attend the roads we must travel in life, and who will pave our paths? Who will heal our souls? Who will bring us back to You in sincere repentance? Who will awaken us from our spiritual sleep, that we may return to You in truth?

Woe unto us in these generations! For we were privileged to behold such awesome and wondrous lights, such pure and radiant lights, that no words or combinations of holy letters could recount their praise, their magnificence, their might, their exaltedness, their loftiness and their splendor!

How many incarnations have we been granted in Your world? How many Heavenly worlds were overturned for our sake? How many miracles and wonders beyond measure did You perform in order to bring to the world such luminaries as these, such holy tzaddikim, such spiritual guides, such teachers of wisdom, such experts in knowledge, such masters of advice! You were with them throughout their holy lives, and You increased Your wonders through them, beyond measure – for many stood up against them every day, but You saved them immediately from all their enemies and persecutors.

In Your extremely hidden and wondrous ways, You did whatever You did, and mercifully preserved them, until they accomplished and acted, began and finished, and performed amazingly new and awesome tikkunim affecting all the worlds, from the highest to the lowest, and healed countless souls – souls of the living and the dead!

You know all these tikkunim and the delight that You derived from the tzaddikim who lived in these generations, from the day the "hidden light" was revealed – the light of Israel and its holy one, scholar and sage, most awesome man of God, our master and teacher, the eminent Rabbi Israel Baal Shem Tov, of blessed memory, who illuminated the face of the earth and established many disciples, holy and awesome tzaddikim and chassidim. He left behind him a blessing,[14] a "planting of his delight,"[15] holy progeny his vitality,[16] the "holy fruit of his loins, more precious than fine gold and pearls,"[17] which all desirable things cannot equal. Together with his disciples and descendants, he revealed Your Godliness in these generations and disseminated Torah among the Jewish people.

They enlightened our eyes and opened our hearts, taught us straight paths, and gave us wondrous advice to come close to You in truth. "Fortunate is the eye that beheld all this!" Is it not for the sake of hearing that our souls grieve?[18] For our entire hope was that they would prolong their days and years in this world, and that we might yet stand before the beauty of their holiness and hear from their awesome mouths more "words of the Living God,"[19] which were new and wondrous every time, when we were privileged to stand before them and hear their words all the days of their holy lives.

However, due to our many sins and our great iniquity, darkness eclipsed the light of our eyes, the desire of our souls. Woe that "the angels overcame the great ones below"[20] and took from us prematurely such awesome "holy arks" as these![21] Woe, what has happened to us! "The crown of our heads has fallen! Woe unto us, for we have sinned!"[22]

Even though we know – we surely know – that even now these tzaddikim are engaged in the tikkun of our souls, nevertheless, it is so bitter for us. For we no longer have the merit to behold their holy faces, to hear their awesome words, to draw from the well of their holy mouths, or to gaze upon their splendor, their beauty, their radiance, and the holy and awesome majesty of their faces, thus to become subsumed within their true grace! Indeed, they were the beauty and grace of the entire world! And whoever was enveloped within their holy grace, within their splendor, within their holy names, could gaze deeply into himself and be truly awakened to return to God!

But now, now, due to our sins, we have lost what we have lost. How much harm sin causes! What will happen now? What can such persecuted people accomplish, such poor and destitute people, such a nation that is "dragged and plucked"[23] – such a poor and destitute nation as Israel? "Therefore, I said, 'Leave me alone, I will weep bitterly!'"[24] My bitter spirit I will assuage, "my voice will resound like the sea,"[25] I will speak and it will be a relief for me. I will speak unto the Lord, God above, come what may.

Master of the Universe, Master of the Universe, Master of the Universe! "You are holy, and awesome is Your Name,"[26] and Your Name is combined with the names of the true tzaddikim! Act for the sake of Your Name, sanctify Your Name, and reveal the truth to the world! Confer merit upon us in Your abundant mercy, and let us know in truth who is the *rosh bayit* in the world today, having been empowered by the true tzaddikim we have mentioned before You. Confer merit upon us, in Your great compassion, so that we might truly draw close to them and be constantly absorbed in the name, beauty and grace of the true tzaddikim. Let us bind ourselves and cleave to them in truth, with a mighty bond that will never break!

Then we will be able to gaze into ourselves and recognize all the character traits and passions that derive from the four elements of fire, air, water and earth,[27] in order to purge them of evil entirely and return to You in wholehearted teshuvah for what occurred in the past. From now on, we will strengthen ourselves with all our might to break and nullify all evil traits and desires from all four elements, and to acquire all virtuous traits. Thus we will serve You constantly in truth, with all our soul and with all our might, until all four elements of our bodies are truly purified and become entirely good, with no admixture of evil at all. All four elements will be transmuted to their supernal source – the four letters of Your holy Name, *YHVH*.

May we gaze deeply into ourselves at all times, take stock of our actions in this lowly world, and examine all our character traits in order to improve, purify and sanctify them to the utmost degree. Let us contemplate the greatness of the Creator and His awesome wonders, for He is doing new and wondrous things every instant; and let us reflect upon ways to perfect the world.

May we draw lofty and pure perceptions from the holy names of the true tzaddikim. From now on, may we succeed in purifying our minds, never allowing our thoughts to wander beyond the bounds of holiness, and even more, never succumbing to evil fantasies, God forbid. May we immerse our minds in the Torah and constantly innovate original and true Torah insights in abundance, according to Your beneficent will.

Let me sanctify my eyes from now on, never again gazing at things that we are forbidden to see, and never even glancing at anything that could lead to lewd thoughts, God forbid. Show me how to conduct myself at all times so that such thoughts and fantasies will not overcome me, due to my very fear of them (as when I overreact by shaking my head or squeezing my eyes shut, as is all too familiar to You). Rather, may I attain true discernment to know how to use my eyes in holiness and purity, according to Your beneficent will, in a manner that will protect me and save me from all evil. Spiritually protect my eyes from now on, in truth, according to Your profound kindness, and help me to refine all four elements with great sanctity. May I continually add holiness upon holiness until I attain absolute goodness.

Then nothing in the world will be able to harm my eyes, wherever I may gaze. No matter what I happen to see, no improper thought of any kind will arise in my mind, and no sight will disturb or upset me. Rather, I will cleave to Your holiness constantly.

Master of the Universe! Help me to attain all this speedily, even though I am so far from all this right now that I am ashamed to entreat You for such things. Yet I trust in Your abundant mercy and rely on the power of the true tzaddikim, and ask that You speedily grant me all this. Indeed, "You can do anything, and nothing can hinder Your objective."[28] You perform miracles in every generation, and nothing is too wondrous for You.

Therefore have compassion toward me, All-Merciful One, abounding in kindness and truth, beneficent beyond measure, magnanimously pardoning sinners and forgiving transgressors, performing acts of charity toward all creatures! Help me, save me, strengthen me and fortify me in Your wondrous ways, so that from now on I may arise every night exactly at chatzot and recite the prayer of Tikkun Chatzot – and mourn, lament and cry profusely over the destruction of the Holy Temple, the House of our holiness and splendor, the House of our life and length of days, the House of our desire, our precious jewel, the glory of our might, our brilliance, our radiance, our beauty and our sanctity! Woe for what has befallen us! Woe that with our sins we brought about the destruction of our Holy Temple, the dwelling place of Your might, the channel for Torah and prayer, and the revelation of Your Divinity! There we were able to attain perceptions of Godliness, to know and perceive You even in this physical world, and to cleave to You forever!

Master of the Universe! Master of the Universe! What's past is past. Our Holy Temple was destroyed long ago, and our tzaddikim passed away, due to our sins. What happened has happened. But over this I surely weep! "Over these I weep; my eyes, my eyes flow with tears!"[29] Due to my many profound and grievous transgressions, both quantitatively and qualitatively, I am responsible for having forestalled the rebuilding of the Holy Temple – and who knows? Perhaps in a previous incarnation, I caused the destruction of the Holy Temple.

Woe unto me for the sins I committed in this life and in other lifetimes! Woe for what have I done, that a foul and despicable person like me destroyed the Holy Temple, delayed its rebuilding, and impeded the redemption of the Jewish people and our return to our Land! Woe unto me that I razed the Holy Temple through my evil deeds, set fire to the Sanctuary, drove the Jewish people into exile among the nations, and prolonged our exile for so long due to my evil and bitter passions!

Master of the Universe! Master of the Universe! Teach me how to cry out before You now! How to bewail my broken and bitter plight now! How to raise my eyes toward You now! How to spend my days in true goodness now!

To where can I flee? To whom can I turn for help? What can I do or accomplish? How can I devote myself to living a true life, in true holiness? How can I save my soul from destruction and escape Your judgment, Your wrath, and Your severe and bitter punishment? How can I spare myself disgrace and shame, now and in the future?

Master of the Universe! Master of the Universe! Act for the sake of Your Name! For the sake of Your glorious

Name, sanctify Your Name! And grant us the merit to magnify and sanctify Your great Name in the world through our deeds!

Merciful One! Master of All! Knower of Hidden Mysteries! You know "all that transpires under the sun,"[30] right now in these generations – how the world has become mixed up and confused beyond all measure. For all the true tzaddikim, glorious ones of the generations, departed from this world in our days, due to our many sins. You alone know their exalted spiritual stature, their might and their holiness, for "Your Name is bound up with their names,"[31] and the more their names are made great, the more Your Name is made great. However, because of our unworthiness, they departed this world before their time. Woe for what has befallen us in these generations! And because of our insensitivity and obtuseness, no one realizes the magnitude of this tragedy and the full ramifications of this terrible blow, this astounding disaster, this "affliction not written in the Torah, which is the death of Torah sages"[32] who perished in our times, due to our sins and transgressions!

Woe unto us for what we have lost! Woe for what has been lost and cannot be found! "The tzaddik perishes, and no one takes it to heart; men of kindness are gathered in, while no one understands that because of the approaching evil the tzaddik was taken away."[33]

Master of the Universe! Master of All! After the damage we incurred through our sins, after causing the destruction of our Holy Temple and the death of the true tzaddikim, help us from now on – so at the very least we may arise each night exactly at chatzot and break our hearts and weep profusely over our enormous sins which produced all this, leaving us like orphans without

ENTERING THE LIGHT

a father, like lost souls that no one seeks, like those who are far that no one tries to bring near, and whose cause no one takes up!

Master of the Universe! Have mercy on us for the sake of Your Name! Behold our lowliness and disgrace! Gaze down from Heaven and see how we have become a laughingstock, a source of derision. Not only are we scorned and downcast among the nations "which arise each day to seek our destruction, but You save us from their hand"[34]; but even among the Jewish people, strife has proliferated to the point that there is bitter contention between our Torah sages. Their hearts are divided against each other, and each is considered despicable and worthless in the sight of his fellow, until we cannot bear it any longer.

Master of the Universe! God full of mercy! Awaken Your compassion toward Your children! Arouse Your inner feelings for us! Have mercy on the remnant of the refugees of Your nation, the House of Israel!

O Merciful One! How can You restrain Yourself from pitying our oppressed souls – the souls of Your people, Israel, who wander the streets, marketplaces and roads? Such precious souls, yet they have been scattered at the head of every street. As the prophet Jeremiah bewailed with repeated laments over each and every soul: "Alas, the gold is dimmed, the exquisite gold is changed! Sacred stones are scattered at the head of every street. The precious children of Zion, comparable to fine gold – alas, they are now treated like earthen jugs, work of a potter's hands!"[35]

Master of the Universe! You alone know the inestimable beauty and holiness of these precious souls, these holy stones, which are now scattered at the head of every street, and no man gathers them up and takes them into his house. Due to our sins, the true tzaddikim have departed – those who are called *rosh bayit*, the "masters of the house" of the world. When they were present in the world and their names were made great, the world had a *rosh bayit* and we all were called *bnei bayit* (family members). But since the day they passed away, due to our sins, and their holy and awesome beauty, splendor and true grace became hidden, we have wandered derelict and bereft; the precious souls of Your people, the House of Israel, are scattered at the head of every street. For the masters of the house of the world have departed, those great tzaddikim who are called *rosh bayit*, and even the faintest trace of their names that remains through their holy books and precious disciples has become obscured through so many layers of concealment, beyond measure.

Meanwhile, the names of famous false leaders who have no connection whatsoever to the Name of God continually become great in the world; indeed, they eclipse the Divine Name. The names of forces outside the domain of holiness prevail, God forbid. Due to our many sins, the world has become so mixed up that we can no longer tell who truly follows God's Torah; whose name derives from the Divine Name, and whose does not; and who is a mixture of both aspects, good and evil, "Luminaries of Light" and "Luminaries of Fire." We do not know what has happened, but our eyes are fixed upon You!

Grant us the privilege of awakening every night precisely at chatzot in order to mourn the destruction of the Holy Temple, which was razed because of our transgressions. In this way, may we awaken Your mercy, so that You will speedily console and gladden our spirits, and for "the mourners of Zion, exchange ashes for splendor."[36] May we subjugate the Luminaries of Fire before the Luminaries of Light. May the holy name – the Divine Name *YHVH*, and the names of the true tzaddikim – prevail over the name of impurity, the names of the outside forces. And may falsehood be nullified before truth.

Let the names of the true tzaddikim be revealed, magnified and publicized throughout the world, as well as their splendor, their beauty, and their holy and awesome grace. May we be deemed worthy to be subsumed within their names and within the splendor of the beauty of their holiness, until our eyes are truly opened. Then we will be able to gaze into ourselves lucidly, into all four elements of the soul, in order to purify, refine and sanctify them from all evil passions and evil traits that derive from them; to sift the evil from the good, and attain all virtuous traits and deeds.

Through the true tzaddikim, confer upon us holy and pure consciousness, until all four levels of the mind[37] and all four elements become incorporated into the holy and awesome, absolutely simple element which is the "*tzaddik yesod olam* – the tzaddik who is the foundation of the world"[38] and the "river that flows from Eden to water the garden."[39]

May everything be incorporated into Your great, holy and awesome Unitary Name, and may You hasten our redemption and rebuild the House of our holiness and splendor! May Your Name, our King, be "magnified, sanctified, blessed, praised, glorified, extolled and lauded"[40] in the mouths of all living creatures constantly, forever and ever!

Enable us to fulfill the mitzvah of tefilin perfectly, with great holiness and purity, with awe and love, with joy and a whole heart, until we draw upon ourselves the splendor of the awesome and holy tefilin. This is the higher consciousness derived from the *rosh bayit*, who fills the "houses" (*batim*) of the tefilin with lofty perceptions – "with wisdom, understanding, knowledge, and all manner of workmanship."[41]

Grant us the privilege of delighting in Shabbat with all our might, celebrating each Shabbat with the greatest joy. Through the holiness of Shabbat, may we also imbue ourselves with the higher consciousness of the *rosh bayit*, the tzaddik who is called "Shabbat of all the days."[42] In this way, we will return to You in truth and become incorporated into Your great Name, which is combined with our names; and we will repair all the damage we have caused to Your great Name.

In Your abundant mercy, protect us and save us from all sicknesses, ailments and diseases that come from the names of impurity and the outside forces, God forbid. These are called "Luminaries of Fire." Heavenly Father, Ruler over all, Eternal Guardian of Israel, protect us and save us from them! May Your great Name stand against them and subjugate, destroy and annihilate the Luminaries of Fire that oppose the Luminaries of Light. Eradicate the names of impurity, the names of the outside forces, and reveal Your holy Name in the world!

Spread over us Your tent of peace in the merit of the holy Shabbat. Guard us, as well as our assets and homes, from all damage and loss, materially and spiritually, all of which derive from the Luminaries of Fire. Save all the houses of Your people, Israel, from fire. O God, protect them always from fire and from all types of damage, for we are incapable of guarding them. On You alone we rely! Have mercy on us and on the entire Jewish people from now on, and protect our houses and property from fire. Do not allow the Luminaries of Fire any dominion over us, God forbid – neither our bodies, nor our souls, nor our wealth. Rather, may we constantly be subsumed within the Luminaries of Light, which in turn are subsumed within Your great Name.

Grant us the privilege of fulfilling the mitzvah of the Four Species perfectly, in its proper time. May we always obtain a beautiful, kosher etrog that possesses every desirable quality; and may You reveal the splendor of the beauty and holiness of Your people, Israel, to the world – particularly the splendor, beauty and holiness of the true tzaddikim and devout Jews – until all humanity longs and yearns to become incorporated into them, to merge into their names and their beauty. All humanity will turn to walk in their ways, thus to perform Your will in truth all their days, forever!

Master of the Universe! Our King and our God! Mercifully fulfill our requests and enable us to attain all that we have asked of You, so that we may truly be incorporated into Your great and holy Name for all eternity! Magnify and sanctify Your great Name through us constantly, and fulfill in us what is written: "Nations shall revere the Name of God, and all earthly kings, Your glory!"[43] "May the Name of God be blessed, now and forever!"[44] "Help us, God of our deliverance, for the sake of the glory of Your Name; save us and atone for our sins for the sake of Your Name!"[45] "Blessed is the Lord, God of Israel, Who alone performs wonders. Blessed is the Name of His glory forever, and may His glory fill all the earth. Amen and amen!"[46]

(LT II, 6)

Notes

1 Jeremiah 31:14, included in Tikkun Chatzot.
2 Lamentations 1:16, included in Tikkun Chatzot.
3 Jeremiah 4:13.
4 Paraphrase of Isaiah 21:3.
5 Paraphrase of Song of Songs 6:1.
6 Lamentations 5:17.
7 I Kings 5:13.
8 For example, see *Zohar* III, 70b. This idea appears repeatedly in the works of the ARI and throughout Kabbalistic and Chassidic literature. Reb Noson discusses it in *Likutey Halakhot, Geviyat Chov MeHaYetomim* 3:19-20; *Apotiki* 5:13-14; *Chezkat Metaltelin* 5:16; *Shluchin* 5:11-13; et passim.
9 See *Likutey Moharan* II, 7; ibid., II, 48, et passim.
10 Jeremiah 31:14.
11 Lamentations 1:2. On a simple level, the expression "her lovers" refers to the surrounding nations to which the Kingdom of Judea turned in a desperate attempt to forge a military alliance (Rashi, ad loc.). Jeremiah allegorizes these alliances as promiscuous relationships, doomed to betrayal and heartbreak.
12 Paraphrase of Isaiah 30:17.
13 Lamentations 5:3.
14 Cf. *Likutey Moharan* II, 7, where Rebbe Nachman states that no tzaddik departs from this world without "leaving behind a blessing" through his children or disciples.
15 Paraphrase of Isaiah 5:7. In Hebrew, the initial letters of *Berakhah Neta Sha'ashu'av* (a blessing, a planting of his delight) possibly

hint to the initials of *Nachman Ben Simchah*, Rebbe Nachman's name and patronymic.
16. A play on Isaiah 6:13: "Like an elm and an oak which, when shedding [their leaves], still have vitality in them, so shall the holy seed be the vitality [of the land]."
17. Paraphrase of Lamentations 4:2.
18. Liturgy, Yom Kippur *Musaf.*
19. *Eruvin* 13b.
20. A figure of speech customarily used to describe the passing of great rabbis and Torah scholars.
21. The Holy Ark is the repository of the Torah scrolls in the synagogue. Reb Noson's phrasing invokes the words of the Talmud: "Those who stand up for a Torah scroll, but not for a Torah scholar, are fools" (*Makkot* 22b).
22. Lamentations 5:16.
23. Paraphrase of Isaiah 18:2.
24. Isaiah 22:4.
25. Paraphrase of Jeremiah 6:23.
26. Liturgy, *Shemoneh Esrei.*
27. See *Mishnat Chassidim, Masekhet Asiyah Gufanit,* ch. 1. The element of fire gives rise to the evil traits of self-importance, arrogance, anger, and pursuit of power and honor. The element of air gives rise to the traits of idle speech, flattery and speaking falsehood. The element of water gives rise to the traits of sensual desire and covetousness. The element of earth gives rise to the traits of laziness and depression. These four elements correspond to the four letters of the Divine Name *YHVH* and the Four Worlds. Rebbe Nachman discusses these concepts in *Likutey Moharan* I, 4:8 and ibid., II, 67, which serves as the basis for this prayer.
28. Job 42:2.
29. Lamentations 1:16.
30. Ecclesiastes 1:13.
31. *Yerushalmi Ta'anit* 2; Rashi on Joshua 7:9; Rashi on Jeremiah 14:7; et al. Rebbe Nachman weaves this theme into his lesson in *Likutey Moharan* II, 66 and 67. In both cases, he relates the Divine Name to Shabbat.

32 *Lamentations Rabbah* 1:37, citing Deuteronomy 28:61. Rebbe Nachman addresses this topic in *Likutey Moharan* I, 57:1.
33 Isaiah 57:1.
34 Pesach Haggadah.
35 Lamentations 4:1-2.
36 Paraphrase of Isaiah 61:3, as found in Tikkun Chatzot. The Hebrew letters *alef, peh, resh*, which spell *EFeR* (ashes) may be recombined to spell *Pe'ER* (splendor).
37 According to the Kabbalah, every person possesses four "mentalities" or levels of the mind with which he can serve God and ultimately perceive Divinity. These levels correspond to the sefirot of Chokhmah, Binah, Da'at and Malkhut.
38 Proverbs 10:25.
39 Genesis 2:10. Rebbe Nachman explains that the tzaddik is called the "foundation of the world" because he is identified with the *Yesod HaPashut*, the Simple Primal Element or "Ground of Being" from which all diversity stems; see *Likutey Moharan* I, 4; ibid., II, 67. The unitary "river that flows from Eden" and subsequently divides into four tributaries symbolizes this paradigm.
40 Liturgy, *Kaddish*.
41 Exodus 35:31.
42 *Zohar* III, 144b.
43 Psalms 102:16.
44 Psalms 113:2.
45 Psalms 79:9.
46 Psalms 72:18-19.

Glossary

Beraita lit., "outside" (Aramaic); indicating a rabbinic teaching that was not redacted by Rabbi Yehudah HaNasi in the Mishnah. In Talmudic debates, a *beraita* does not have the same authority as a teaching from the Mishnah.

Chametz leavened products such as bread, crackers, noodles and cookies, which are forbidden on Pesach

Chatzot midnight. According to Rebbe Nachman, this period of Divine grace begins six hours after halakhic nightfall (*tzeit hakokhavim*, the appearance of three medium-sized stars in the nighttime sky) and lasts for two hours. For more details, see *The Sweetest Hour* (Breslov Research Institute).

Da'at higher perception; Divine knowledge. When capitalized, refers to one of the ten sefirot.

Dayan (pl. ***dayanim***) rabbi empowered to serve on a *bet din* (rabbinical court) and render decisions in legal cases

Deveykut cleaving of the soul to God

Erev the day before; e.g., Erev Shabbat is Friday, Erev Pesach is the day before Pesach begins

Four Species the lulav (palm branch), aravot (willows), hadasim (myrtles) and etrog (citron), which are taken together and waved in all directions during the holiday of Sukkot. On the most basic level, waving the Four Species relates to our prayers for sufficient rainfall during the rest of the year. On a mystical level, this rite transmits Divine knowledge to our hearts, and from thence to the entire world (e.g., see *Likutey Moharan* I, 33).

Gehinnom hell; the purification process which the soul must endure after death in order to become capable of experiencing the bliss of the World to Come

Gematria a system of calculating the numerical value of Hebrew letters and words, used in rabbinic and Kabbalistic writings to explore the Torah's hidden meanings

GLOSSARY

Hakafot circular dances performed in the synagogue, especially on the holidays of Sukkot and Shemini Atzeret/Simchat Torah

Hallel psalms recited after the *Shemoneh Esrei* prayer on Yom Tov, in commemoration of the psalms recited by the Levites in the Holy Temple

Kavanah (pl. ***kavanot***) concentration; intention. In Kabbalistic practice, the mystical meanings which one contemplates while performing the mitzvot, or specific spiritual effects that a person wishes to accomplish through his devotions.

Kelipah (pl. ***kelipot***) lit., "husk"; in Kabbalistic thought, an unholy force that surrounds and conceals the sparks of holiness (the various aspects of holiness and spiritual vitality present in Creation)

Keruvim two winged, angelic forms made of gold which adorned the Holy Ark in both the Tabernacle and the Holy Temple. According to the sages, the space between the *Keruvim* served as the channel for prophecy.

Kinot prayers of lamentation, such as those customarily recited in the synagogue on Tisha B'Av evening and morning

Korban Pesach the Pesach offering, a yearling lamb that was ritually slaughtered at the Holy Temple in Jerusalem after midday on Erev Pesach, then roasted and eaten in the evening during the Pesach Seder.

Mashiach the Jewish Messiah, a patrilineal descendant of King David who will rule the world in benevolence and peace, and teach Divine wisdom, at the End of Days; see *Mishneh Torah, Shoftim*, Laws of Kings, ch. 11, 12

Mikveh a gathering of water (e.g., an ocean, pool, stream or man-made pool built to halakhic specifications) used for ritual purification

Mitzvah (pl. ***mitzvot***) a Torah commandment; religious precept

Musaf additional prayer service conducted on Shabbat and festival mornings, commemorating the Additional Offering given in the Holy Temple at that time

Nefesh ▪ lower soul, which animates the body

Neshamah ▪ higher soul, seat of the intellect

Other Side ▪ (Aramaic: *Sitra Achra*), the *Zohar*'s term for the realm of evil. This usage reflects the principle that God created a dualistic universe in which holiness and impurity, good and evil, right and wrong, darkness and light, etc., offset one another to give man freedom of choice.

Pesach ▪ the biblical festival of Passover

Rosh Bayit ▪ master of the house

Rosh Chodesh ▪ first day of each Hebrew month

Ru'ach ▪ spirit or vital soul, seat of the emotions

Sefirah (pl. ***sefirot***) ▪ One of the ten Divine emanations through which all entities on all levels of Creation came into being and are continually recreated *ex nihilo*. These emanations are: Keter (Crown), Chokhmah (Wisdom), Binah (Understanding), [Da'at (Knowledge)], Chesed (Kindness), Gevurah (Might), Tiferet (Beauty), Netzach (Victory), Hod (Splendor), Yesod (Foundation) and Malkhut (Kingship).

Sefirat HaOmer ▪ The counting of forty-nine days between the holidays of Pesach and Shavuot, a time of spiritual preparation for the transforming event of Receiving the Torah at Mount Sinai. In Kabbalistic thought, these forty-nine days correspond to seven aspects of each of the seven lower sefirot, culminating in the fiftieth day of Shavuot, which expresses the full revelation of God's Kingship.

Shabbat ▪ the Jewish Sabbath, beginning at sundown on Friday and ending on Saturday night with the appearance of three medium-sized stars in the nighttime sky

Shefa ▪ efflux or influx, depending on context. In Chassidic thought, a transmission of Divine energy and blessing that manifests itself in various ways, spiritually and materially

Shekhinah ▪ the immanent Divine Presence which animates and sustains Creation; sometimes identified with the sefirah of Malkhut

GLOSSARY

Shemoneh Esrei lit., "Eighteen Blessings," the key text of the three daily prayer services redacted more than two thousand years ago by the Men of the Great Assembly. A nineteenth blessing was added during the Talmudic era to beseech God's salvation from informers and heretics.

Sukkah a thatch-covered structure of three or four walls used as a residence during the festival of Sukkot

Teshuvah lit., "return"; repentance

Tikkun (pl. ***tikkunim***) repair, perfection, correction, rectification

Tikkun Chatzot The Midnight Lament, a special order of prayers mourning the destruction of the Holy Temple. See *The Sweetest Hour* (Breslov Research Institute).

Tzaddik (pl. ***tzaddikim***) righteous person. In Chassidic thought, one who has purified his heart of all evil, making himself a channel for Divine revelation and true compassion

Tzedakah charity

Tzimtzum (pl. ***tzimtzumim***) constriction

Yahrtzeit anniversary of the date of death

Yom Tov Jewish festival

Publications

Following are selected publications of Breslov Research Institute. A complete color catalog is available upon request.

WORKS BY AND ABOUT REBBE NACHMAN

Rebbe Nachman was an original Chassidic thinker and spiritual leader whose teachings span the ages. These works present the scope and significance of his lessons on all subjects.

THE ALEPH-BET BOOK
Translated by Moshe Mykoff

Throughout his life, Rebbe Nachman penned succinct, powerful and challenging epigrams distilling the wisdom of the Torah for every area of life, spiritual and physical. Calling his collection, "my dearly beloved friend," the Rebbe used these epigrams to inspire himself along the path that led him to greatness.

CROSSING THE NARROW BRIDGE: A Practical Guide to Rebbe Nachman's Teachings
by Chaim Kramer
Edited by Moshe Mykoff

Rebbe Nachman said: "The world is a very narrow bridge. The main thing is not to be afraid." This upbeat, down-to-earth book gives clear, detailed guidance for applying Rebbe Nachman's teachings to our everyday lives. Exploring a broad range of topics – from joy, peace and charity to earning a living, taking care of one's health, and raising children – this work answers many of the practical and technical questions that puzzle those who are making their first acquaintance with Breslov teachings.

LIKUTEY MOHARAN (multi-volume)
Translated by Moshe Mykoff
Annotated by Chaim Kramer

The first authoritative translation of Rebbe Nachman's magnum opus, containing all his major lessons. Presented with facing Hebrew text, full explanatory notes, source references and supplementary information, plus a variety of charts which assist the reader with Kabbalistic teachings found in the text. Volume I contains Reb Noson's introduction to the original work, brief biographies of Rebbe Nachman and Reb Noson, and a bibliography.

RABBI NACHMAN'S STORIES
Translated by Rabbi Aryeh Kaplan

Our sages told stories to convey some of the deepest secrets about God and His relationship to the world. Rebbe Nachman developed this ancient art to perfection. The Rebbe's allegorical stories are richly structured and deeply insightful, while containing all the ingredients of a marvelously entertaining read. Rabbi Kaplan adds a masterful running commentary drawn from the works of Rebbe Nachman's students, giving English-speaking readers access to authentic interpretations of these stories for the first time.

RABBI NACHMAN'S WISDOM
Translated by Rabbi Aryeh Kaplan
Edited by Rabbi Zvi Aryeh Rosenfeld

This classic work presents Rebbe Nachman's everyday conversations and fundamental teachings on everything from faith, joy and meditation to Kabbalistic insights. The conversations were recorded verbatim by his leading disciple, Reb Noson, producing a vivid picture of the atmosphere surrounding the Rebbe, his wit, directness and wisdom. Also included is an account of Rebbe Nachman's adventure-filled pilgrimage to the Holy Land at the height of the Napoleonic wars in 1798.

TZADDIK
Translated by Avraham Greenbaum

An intimate biographical portrait of Rebbe Nachman by the one who knew him best – Reb Noson, his closest disciple. Containing numerous conversations and a variety of the Rebbe's sayings, stories, dreams and visions, this work gives readers a clearer picture of who Rebbe Nachman was and the import of his teachings.

BIOGRAPHY / HISTORY

Works exploring the lives of Rebbe Nachman and Reb Noson, and the history of the Breslov movement.

PUBLICATIONS

AGAINST ALL ODDS
By Gedaliah Fleer

For nearly fifty years, the Communists barred access to the city of Uman, burial site of Rebbe Nachman of Breslov. The situation looked hopeless – until a young American chassid set out to pray at the Rebbe's grave, no matter what obstacles stood in his way. This true, action-packed adventure story brings the reader face to face with the surveillance, scare tactics and undercover activities of Communist Russia in the 1960s – and the heroism of Breslover chassidim trapped behind the Iron Curtain.

THROUGH FIRE AND WATER: The Life of Reb Noson of Breslov
By Chaim Kramer
Edited by Avraham Greenbaum

Why did Rebbe Nachman's followers never choose another rebbe? How has the Breslov movement survived and flourished for nearly two hundred years? To find the answer, meet Reb Noson, the Rebbe's closest disciple, who devoted his life to bringing the Rebbe's message of faith, hope and joy to the world. Defying opposition from his own family and persecution by other chassidic movements, Reb Noson single-handedly ensured the continuation of the Breslov movement for centuries to come. This thoroughly-researched biography will keep you absorbed for hours as you relive Reb Noson's life step by step. Includes full background information, maps and indices.

UNTIL THE MASHIACH: The Life of Rabbi Nachman
By Rabbi Aryeh Kaplan
Edited by Rabbi Dovid Shapiro

This definite account of Rebbe Nachman's life traces his career in rich detail, day by day and year by year. Features an extensive historical overview, detailed maps, and full appendices listing significant towns and cities, biographical data, and anecdotes about Rebbe Nachman's family, students and other contemporary figures, with full source references throughout.

INSPIRATIONAL

The essence of Rebbe Nachman's mission was to give practical guidance for spiritual growth. These works offer advice and encouragement for today's spiritual seeker.

PUBLICATIONS

ADVICE
Translated by Avraham Greenbaum

"The main thing is not the learning, but the doing," say the sages. In spiritual matters, the basic question is, "How?" How to have faith? How to pray? To develop trust? To show love? To achieve happiness? This translation of Reb Noson's *Likutey Etzot* collects Rebbe Nachman's practical guidance and teachings on all aspects of life, subject by subject.

RABBI NACHMAN'S TIKKUN
Translated by Avraham Greenbaum

Depression, one of the greatest illnesses of modern times, can be traced to man's abuse of his God-given powers. Rebbe Nachman revealed a wondrous antidote – the Tikkun HaKlali (General Remedy) – which attacks the flaw by drawing on the most creative force in the universe: song. This volume of insight and commentary includes the Shemot HaTzaddikim (Names of the Tzaddikim), the recital of which arouses powerful spiritual forces.

RESTORE MY SOUL
Translated by Avraham Greenbaum

"No situation is so desperate that it cannot be turned to good." This is a book for people in all walks of life. It contains extracts from the entire corpus of Breslov writings to combat hopelessness and depression, and to draw from the wellsprings of joy and spiritual strength.

EXPLORATIONS

Each of these works highlights Rebbe Nachman's teachings on a specific theme.

ANATOMY OF THE SOUL
By Chaim Kramer with Avraham Sutton

Since man was created "in the image of God," each organ of the human body has a spiritual as well as a physical meaning. This fascinating study uncovers the mystical connection between each aspect of the human body – the skeletal and muscular system, the circulatory and respiratory systems, the reproductive system, etc. – and the Ten Sefirot, as well as the five levels of the soul. Heighten your awareness of the awesome spiritual power you have at your fingertips – and in all other limbs as well.

PUBLICATIONS

AZAMRA! / AYEH?

Rebbe Nachman said: "It is a great mitzvah to be happy always." In *Azamra!* (I will sing!), the Rebbe points the way to happiness – by finding the "good points" in ourselves and others. His original lesson is accompanied by a selection of explanatory material which demonstrates both the depth of his teaching and its application in everyday life.

To achieve lasting happiness, you have to know how to rise out of the lows. This is the theme of Rebbe Nachman's *Ayeh?* (Where?), which shows how to find hope in even the darkest, most desperate situations.

GARDEN OF THE SOULS: Rebbe Nachman on Suffering
By Avraham Greenbaum

One of Rebbe Nachman's most beautiful and evocative teachings, this lesson offers guidance and comfort for dealing with pain and suffering in our own lives and the lives of those around us. Faith makes it possible to find meaning in the trials of this world, and to turn all challenges into opportunities for elevation and profound joy.

THIS LAND IS MY LAND: History, Conflict and Hope in the Land of Israel
By Chaim Kramer

God promised Abraham and his descendants the Land of Israel – but at what price? Did God intend for us to fight never-ending wars with our enemies, pay the high price of terrorism, and suffer from international bad press? This contemporary work views the Promised Land through a truly unique historical lens, using the lessons of the Bible, the Talmud and the Kabbalah, as expounded in the teachings of Rebbe Nachman, to discover genuine, non-political solutions to Israel's plight – and the possibility for a true and lasting peace.

TSOHAR / MAYIM

Even in life's worst entanglements, there's always an exit – by taking the route of simple, honest truth. Rebbe Nachman's *Tsohar* (Light) teaches us how to bring light into all situations and illuminate the path to our real selves.

Rebbe Nachman explores the idea of free will in *Mayim* (Water), based on his arresting interpretation of the Talmudic account of the four sages who entered Paradise. There may be many lies, but there is only one truth.

SELF-HELP

Books to read again and again to master the tools for self-actualization.

HEALING LEAVES: Prescriptions for Inner Strength, Meaning and Hope
Compiled by Yitzchok Leib Bell

This volume collects, for the first time, the inspiring words and advice disseminated by Reb Noson of Breslov in the many letters he wrote to his son and disciples. Arranged by subject, Reb Noson's encouraging missives are needed even more today, as they provide answers for those of us seeking to bring real meaning and hope into our lives.

HIDDEN TREASURES: How to Realize Your Potential
By Chaim Kramer with Yitzchok Bell

What made Rebbe Nachman different from many other Chassidic masters was his ability to access the mysteries of the Kabbalah and extract practical advice for living life to the fullest. Here the Rebbe elucidates one of the first secrets of Creation – how God went about creating the world as we know it – and applies its lessons to our own quest for physical, financial, emotional and spiritual success. An invaluable guide for achieving personal greatness.

THE EMPTY CHAIR
Adapted by Moshe Mykoff

A treasury of insights and advice for living joyously and spiritually, designed for people of all faiths – and even of no faith. With timeless wisdom, Rebbe Nachman shows us how to fill the empty chair – the alienated self – by leaving sadness and embracing hope and joy.

PRAYER

Rebbe Nachman emphasized prayer – both structured and spontaneous – as the main way to come close to God.

PUBLICATIONS

THE FIFTIETH GATE (multi-volume)
Likutey Tefilot – **Reb Noson's prayers**
Translated by Avraham Greenbaum

There are times when we yearn to communicate with God but don't know what to say. We can find ourselves in the expressive and eloquent prayers of Reb Noson, which are based on the teachings in Rebbe Nachman's *Likutey Moharan*. Unique in Jewish spiritual literature, *Likutey Tefilot* includes prayers and supplications on every topic, suiting all moods and needs. Volume I includes a full introduction to the concept of prayer and its centrality in Jewish life.

THE FLAME OF THE HEART
Translated by Dovid Sears

Translations of selected prayers from *Likutey Tefilot* on a variety of topics, including: Finding God in Everything; Awakening the Soul; Midnight Meditation; Simplicity; Grasping the Infinite; Unity in Diversity; Beginning Anew; Love of Humanity; Hospitality; Spiritual Ups and Downs.

THE GENTLE WEAPON: Prayers for Everyday and Not-So-Everyday Moments
Adapted by Moshe Mykoff and S. C. Mizrahi

Life makes warriors of us all. To emerge victorious, we must arm ourselves with the most potent of weapons: prayer. These soul-stirring prayers strengthen the heart while bringing us closer to God and a deeper understanding of ourselves.

THE SWEETEST HOUR: Tikkun Chatzot
Compiled and translated by Avraham Greenbaum

In Jewish tradition, the wee hours of the night are especially propitious for contemplation of the Jewish exile and yearning for redemption, both collective and personal. This book explains the meaning and purpose of Tikkun Chatzot (the Midnight Lament) and contains the first complete English translation of this inspiring service, together with detailed instructions for when and how to say it.

OUTPOURING OF THE SOUL
Translated by Rabbi Aryeh Kaplan

"When the summer begins to approach, go out to meditate in the meadows. When every bush of the field begins to return to life and grow, they all yearn to be included in your prayer." With these words, Rebbe Nachman gave pride of place to the spontaneous, improvised prayer uttered in one's own language and words – hitbodedut. This handbook of the Rebbe's teachings on prayer includes Rabbi Kaplan's scholarly introduction placing hitbodedut in the context of the history of Jewish prayer and meditation.

WHERE EARTH AND HEAVEN KISS:
A Guide to Rebbe Nachman's Path of Meditation
By Ozer Bergman

This easy-to-follow, how-to guide walks the reader through the practice of hitbodedut in all times and situations, offering encouragement and advice for each step of the process. It also presents many ideas and scripts that can enhance any hitbodedut session, including the original "One-Minute Hitbodedut."

FESTIVALS

Insights into the meaning of Jewish holidays and seasons of the year.

THE BRESLOV HAGGADAH
Compiled and translated by Rabbi Yehoshua Starret and
Chaim Kramer

The classic Pesach Haggadah, accompanied by Rebbe Nachman's insights and other commentary drawn from Breslov and general sources. Includes the story of the Exodus and Pesach anecdotes, plus Rebbe Nachman's teachings about Chol HaMoed, the counting of the Omer, and the holiday of Shavuot.

ESTHER: A Breslov Commentary on the Megillah
Compiled and adapted by Rabbi Yehoshua Starret

This commentary on the Book of Esther "unmasks" the drama of Shushan that takes place within each one of us at this very moment! How does Haman's plot translate into modern terms? How does Esther – the radiant Jewish soul – rise to the challenge? And where do we find Mordekhai – true leadership – today? This work includes the full Hebrew text of the Megillah and insights into the meaning of Purim and its mitzvot – gifts to the poor, gifts to friends, the festive meal and joyous insobriety.

PUBLICATIONS

SHABBAT ZEMIROT AND BIRKAT HAMAZON
Compiled by Rabbi Yehoshua Starret

An essential companion for the Shabbat table, this elegant, full-color volume contains the entire text of blessings and songs for all Shabbat meals, in Hebrew with facing English translation. Interspersed within the text of each meal are Breslov insights into Shabbat customs and rituals, and anecdotes from Rebbe Nachman's own Shabbat table, giving the reader a richer and more satisfying "taste" of Shabbat.

UMAN! UMAN! ROSH HASHANAH!

"Whether you eat or don't eat, whether you sleep or don't sleep, whether you pray or don't pray, just make sure to be with me for Rosh HaShanah, no matter what!" Rebbe Nachman exhorted his followers. Today, more than 20,000 people stream to the Ukrainian city of Uman at Rosh HaShanah to fulfill the Rebbe's request. This booklet explains the significance of the annual pilgrimage, the concept of the tzaddik and the meaning of Rosh HaShanah, and offers practical tips for registering and preparing for the trip.

www.ingramcontent.com/pod-product-compliance
Lightning Source LLC
Chambersburg PA
CBHW061633040426
42446CB00010B/1390